The Ultimate
Low-Carb
Cookbook

The Ultimate
Low-Carb
Cookbook

150 Delectable Recipes

Mary B. Johnson

Photography by Michael Cogliantry

BARNES
&NOBLE
BOOKS
NEW YORK

10 9 8 7 6 5 4 3 2 1

Library of Congress Cataloging-in-Publication data
available upon request

Published by Sterling Publishing Co., Inc.
387 Park Avenue South, New York, NY 10016
© 2004 by Sterling Publishing Co., Inc.
Exclusively for Barnes & Noble Books

Photographs ©2004 by Michael Cogliantry
Food Stylist: Toni Brogan
Prop Stylist: Lynda White

Design by Liz Trovato
Manufactured in China
All rights reserved

Photograph on opposite overleaf: *Party Pickled Shrimp* (see page 31
for recipe)

ISBN: 0-7607-5570-1

Contents

Introduction

As a nutritionist and a passionate chef, I am fascinated by the relationship between a country's native cuisine and the role food plays within its culture. I have noted on my trips to Asia, particularly, that moderate portions of foods packed with fresh ingredients, bold flavors, and a sparse amount of sugar make for incredibly healthy and delicious meals (and invariably lead to reed-like hips!).

This cookbook is a collection of some of my favorite recipes from my friends, family, cooking classes, and travels across the country and around the world. All these recipes, in their original state or with a little tweaking, contain 10 or fewer grams of carbohydrates per serving, so doing the math of meal-planning should be easy. There are no special dietary products used; these are not diet recipes, just delicious ones that happen to be low-carb.

As an easy weight-gainer, I have pondered the current popularity of a low-carbohydrate diet and the near certainty that the weight lost will be regained once the dieter returns to the old way of eating. I hope this book will help you lose pounds, but more importantly, that it will help you leave behind the carb-oriented palate and cooking repertoire that caused the problem in the first place.

I once read about a woman who vowed that when the mileage on her exercise bike reached the distance from her house to Australia, she'd fly there in celebration of her feat. I hope that your weight loss from cooking with these recipes will inspire some similar creative success story involving far away places. By the time you've finished with the book, you will have a new palate and pantry, probably an assortment of exotic small cups and plates for glamorizing your table, and if not reed-like hips, smaller ones than you started with!

The Low-Carb Lowdown

There are three basic elements of food—fat, protein, and carbohydrates. The United States Department of Agriculture (USDA) developed a research-based plan showing the relative importance of these elements in various foods. This Food Pyramid outlines what to eat each day and is proposed to serve as a general guideline for helping

Opposite page: Grilled Leek and Gruyère Frittata, (see page 173)

you create a healthful diet that accommodates your food preferences. The Food Pyramid emphasizes on controlling fat intake, because most Americans eat diets too high in fat, especially saturated fat. That means a higher intake of carbohydrates and a smaller intake of protein and fat. Not everyone, however, is aware of the good-carb, bad-carb distinction. Carbohydrates are a necessary part of a healthy diet because they provide the body with the energy it needs for physical activity and to keep organs functioning properly. Many foods rich in whole-grain carbohydrates are also good sources of essential vitamins and minerals.

The USDA Food Pyramid is slightly oversimplified in that it does not distinguish between different types of fats or different types of carbohydrates. It is based on the old mantra that "fat is bad" and its corollary, "carbohydrates are good." Actually, there are good fats and bad fats. The worst fats of all are the partially hydrogenated trans fats that are ubiquitous in margarine, shortening, and most store-bought baked goods. Saturated fats were not found to be as bad as once thought. But monounsaturated fats, found in nuts and olive oil, are good for you, as are the essential omega-3 fatty acids found in fish and flaxseed. There are also differences among carbohydrates. Starches, sugars, and processed grains, which provide little or no nutritional value, are not nearly as healthful as high-fiber foods. The latter are far more nutritionally sound.

Prolonging life and preventing disease are essential factors in the consideration of a diet plan. It has been proven that excess pounds make people sluggish, lethargic, unmotivated, and generally hinder the course you need to take towards a long and healthy life. It is on this point that the plethora of diets out there are providing conflicting information about what is a "healthy" way to lose and maintain weight. The Atkins, Zone, and high-protein diets have proven that, if followed exactly, they can promote weight loss.

Ultimately, the percentage of protein you need will depend on whether or not you are dieting. If, for instance, you're on a 1,200 calorie a day diet and want to lose weight, and you're only eating 10 percent protein, you're not getting enough protein to support lean tissue. Even 20 percent isn't enough to support lean tissue. Studies have shown that you need to consume at least 76 grams of protein daily;

therefore, you should tend toward consuming the higher amounts of protein recommended for a 1,200 calorie per day diet.

But many experts do stop short of recommending the very high levels of protein suggested by eating plans like the Atkins diet because these plans so drastically cut carbohydrates—the initial phase of the Atkins diet limits carbohydrates to 20 grams a day. That's because carbohydrates are the major source of fiber in the diet. Just cutting carbohydrates back to, say, 50 percent of your diet might be enough, and would still allow for enough carbs to be within the range recommended by the American Dietetic Association. The idea is to increase lean protein and decrease carbohydrates, all the time striving for a really healthy mix that will satiate your hunger and not leave you feeling deprived of certain foods.

Health, Carbs, and the Glycemic Index

Traditionally, carbohydrates that were classified as complex carbohydrates—such as bread, pasta, and other starches—were considered to be "good," and simple carbohydrates or sugars—such as table sugar, candy, and honey—were thought of as "bad." More recently, however, another system for classifying carbohydrates has received a great deal of attention, calling into question many of the old assumptions about how carbohydrates relate to health. This system, known as the glycemic index, measures how quickly and how strongly blood sugar rises after a person eats a food that contains carbohydrates. Diets filled with high-glycemic-index foods, which cause quick and strong increases in blood sugar levels, have been linked to an increased risk for both diabetes and heart disease.

A number of factors determine a food's glycemic index. One of the most important is how highly processed its carbohydrates are. In highly processed carbohydrates, the outer bran and inner germ layer are removed from the original kernel of grain, which causes bigger spikes in blood sugar levels after consumption than would occur with less-processed grains. Whole-grain foods tend to have a lower glycemic index than their more highly processed counterparts. For example, white rice, which is highly processed, has a higher glycemic index than brown rice, which is less highly processed.

The number of grams of carbohydrates allowed per day varies

greatly among individuals. Some people need to keep their carb count to 20 grams or less per day to lose weight. Others may successfully lose weight on 50 or 60 grams per day. Non-obese diabetics may eat as much as 100 grams of complex carbs per day. But remember, just because you are allowed to eat 20 grams (or 50, or 60) of carbs per day doesn't mean that you should eat those in the form of sugar or starch. Make sure every gram of carbohydrate you eat is in the form of healthier complex carbohydrates found in vegetables or whole grains. And be especially careful that your carbohydrates come from foods that have a low glycemic index.

Counting carbohydrate grams is necessary for a low-carb plan, but you mustn't lose sight of the bigger picture. You need to become sensitive to, and aware of, what makes up your daily food intake—the type of carb, the type of fat—and then shoot for a realistic standard such as 20 carbohydrate grams per serving. If your carb total per meal becomes greater than you are comfortable with, then make ingredient substitutions, always trying to create a balance.

The Ultimate Low-Carb Cookbook provides recipes that ensure higher-protein and good-fat intake while reducing your ingestion of carbohydrates. Most importantly, these recipes won't make you feel as if you are on a diet. Their bold combinations of fresh ingredients and flavorful herbs and spices offer interesting and satisfying tastes as well as looking beautiful on the plate.

Appetizers

Triple-Radish Chips

The French have a variety of radishes grown for eating with butter at breakfast. You can share the taste experience with these stylish appetizers.

3 tablespoons unsalted butter, softened

2 tablespoons minced shallot or chives

2 teaspoons balsamic vinegar or more to taste

pinch of fine sea salt or more to taste

1 cup coarsely shredded radishes

32 (1/4 inch thick) slices from large radishes

radish sprouts for garnish

▪ Mix butter, shallot, vinegar, and salt in medium bowl until blended. Fold in shredded radishes. Taste and adjust seasoning. Spread over radish slices; sprinkle with sprouts.

Per serving: 11 calories, trace carbohydrates, trace protein, 1 g fat

(See overleaf for recipe photo)

Spicy Toasted Almonds

MAKES ABOUT 30 SERVINGS

Born to be nibbled, nuts are addictive at cocktail parties. These are lightly spiced.

4 tablespoons butter, melted
4 cups whole blanched almonds
1 tablespoon salt

1/2 teaspoon hot paprika, cayenne
    pepper, or hot curry powder

■ Preheat oven to 325° F. Place butter and nuts in a medium bowl and toss to coat. Spread the nuts in one layer in a shallow baking pan or cookie sheet and bake for 25 minutes, shaking the pan and stirring the nuts two or three times while baking to prevent scorching. Cool nuts in pan and sprinkle with salt and paprika. Toss to coat. Store in airtight container.

Per serving: 126 calories, 4 g carbohydrates, 4 g protein, 11 g fat

Cajun Cheese Wafers

MAKES ABOUT 24 WAFERS

These cheese rounds make a delicious and satisfying snack.

8 ounces extra-sharp cheddar cheese, cut into 1/2-inch cubes

3 tablespoons Cajun Spice Rub, (see page 98)
3 tablespoons unsalted butter

▓ Place cheese in plastic food-storage bag. Add spice mix; shake to coat. Melt and spread 1 tablespoon butter on nonstick griddle over medium heat, When butter foam subsides, place one third of cheese cubes about 2 inches apart on griddle. Cook 2 minutes, until cheese melts and forms a browned, crisp round. Remove to paper towels to drain. Repeat with remaining cheese and butter.

Per serving: 51 calories, trace carbohydrates, 2 g protein, 5 g fat

Spanish-Style Marinated Black Olives

MAKES 24 SERVINGS (1 1/2 CUPS)

These are perfect with a glass of wine.

2 garlic cloves, crushed through a press
2 tablespoons sherry vinegar
1/2 to 1 teaspoon sweet, bittersweet, or hot Spanish paprika (to taste)

1 pound large ripe olives such as Greek Kalamata, pitted
1/2 lemon, thinly sliced

■ Combine garlic, vinegar, and 1/2 teaspoon paprika in large bowl; mix until blended. Add olives and lemon slices; toss to mix. Taste and add more paprika if desired. Place in jar; marinate at room temperature for at least a week, stirring occasionally.

Per serving: 28 calories, 3 g carbohydrates, trace protein, 2 g fat

Blue Cheese–Walnut 'wiches

MAKES 10 SERVINGS

You can easily make these open-faced 'wiches.

20 perfect, fat walnut halves
2¹/₂ ounces blue cheese, softened

■ Preheat oven to 325° F. Spread out the walnuts in a small roasting pan and bake, stirring after 4 minutes, until fragrant and sizzling, about 8 minutes. Pour out onto a plate and set aside.

■ Slice the cheese into 10 equal-size chunks. Sandwich each cheese slice between two walnut halves, with the flat sides of the nuts facing towards the center. Place on a small serving tray.

Per serving: 58 calories, trace carbohydrates, 2 g protein, 5 g fat

A Quintet of Yogurt-Cheese Spreads

MAKES 16 SERVINGS

Use any number of the Yogurt-Cheese Spread variations to create a bright and flavorful platter.

Yogurt Cheese, (see page 170)
1/4 cup best-quality extra-virgin
   olive oil, or more if needed

Sliced vegetables and Belgian
   endive leaves for serving

■ Mound cheese on a large shallow platter to maximize the surface for seasoning; drizzle with oil. Use as a spread for vegetables.

Per serving: 66 calories, 4 g carbohydrates, 3 g protein, 4 g fat

Variations

Fresh Herb Spread: Sprinkle cheese with 1 teaspoon each chopped fresh rosemary, thyme, and oregano.

Cracked Mixed-Pepper Spread: Sprinkle cheese with 1 teaspoon each freshly ground black, green, and pink peppercorns instead of herbs.

Garlic and Parsley Spread: Stir 2 garlic cloves that have been crushed through a press and 1/4 cup freshly chopped parsley into finished cheese before placing on platter.

Roasted Garlic and Red Pepper Spread: Mash Roasted Garlic to taste, (see page 100), and mix with 1/4 cup finely chopped roasted red peppers into finished cheese before placing on platter.

Per serving: 80 calories, 4 carbohydrates, 4 g protein, 4 g fat

Parmesan Pecans

MAKES ABOUT 15 SERVINGS

With their naturally sweet meatiness, pecans are interestingly seasoned in ways other nuts can't be. These will go quickly.

nonstick cooking spray
1/2 cup freshly grated Parmesan
   cheese
1 teaspoon dried parsley flakes
1/2 teaspoon dried Italian herb
   seasoning

1/2 teaspoon garlic salt
dash cayenne pepper
1 egg white
2 cups pecan halves

▓ Preheat oven to 250F degrees. Grease large baking sheet with cooking spray.

▓ Mix cheese, herbs, garlic salt, and cayenne in medium bowl; beat egg white until frothy in another medium bowl. Add pecans to egg white, tossing to coat. Drain nuts slightly and add to cheese mixture. Toss to coat. Spread in single layer on prepared baking sheet; bake 30 minutes, until golden and crisp, stirring occasionally.

Per 1-ounce serving: 123 calories, 2 g carbohydrates, 3 g protein, 12 g fat

Fonduta with Roasted Garlic

MAKES 24 SERVINGS (ABOUT 2 CUPS)

The Swiss have nothing on the Italians when it comes to melting cheese. This dip can easily be used as a sauce for a bowl of steamed vegetables.

Roasted Garlic, (see page 100)
3/4 cup dry white wine (preferably Italian) or vegetable broth
1 pound Italian fontina cheese, shredded

freshly ground white pepper to taste
blanched cauliflower and broccoli florets (about 2 cups of each)

■ Squeeze roasted garlic from each clove into bowl and mash with fork or place in blender or food processor and puree.

■ Heat wine or broth in heavy saucepan over medium heat until hot but not boiling. Add handfuls of the cheese, stirring constantly with wooden spoon, until cheese melts and mixture is smooth. Stir in garlic puree to taste and season with pepper. Serve in fondue pot over canned heat, with short bamboo skewers for dipping vegetables.

Per serving: 91 calories, 3 g carbohydrates, 6 g protein, 6 g fat

Bay Scallop Seviche with Avocado

MAKES 8 SERVINGS

The power of acid to "cook" protein without heat is amazing. A little sweet, buttery avocado is the perfect foil for the sour marinade.

1 pound bay scallops
1 fresh hot red pepper, finely diced
6 garlic chives, minced
1/2 cup fresh lime juice

1/2 cup fresh lemon juice
1 ripe avocado
chopped fresh cilantro for garnish

■ Combine scallops, pepper, chives, lime juice, and lemon juice in a shallow glass bowl; toss to coat. Cover; refrigerate 4 hours, until scallops lose their translucence.

■ To serve: Peel, pit and slice avocado into 8 wedges; place 1 slice on each of 8 small plates. Top with drained scallops. Sprinkle with cilantro.

Per serving: 88 calories, 5 g carbohydrates, 10 g protein, 3 g fat

Salt Cod Dip with Roasted Garlic and Celeriac

(Brandade de Morue)

MAKES 10 SERVINGS

This warm French classic is usually made with potatoes, but the delicate celery flavor of celeriac makes an interesting variation.

1 pound salt cod
2 large celeriac bulbs (about 1 pound each)
8 large cloves Roasted Garlic, (see page 100)
1/3 cup best-quality extra-virgin olive oil

1/2 cup heavy cream or more if needed
freshly ground white pepper to taste
Belgian endive leaves for dipping

▣ Soak cod in a bowl of cool water overnight, changing water every 3 hours. Taste cod after 24 hours; it should be tender and tasty. (Do not oversoak.) Rinse and drain; cut into 1-inch chunks. Pat dry with clean tea towels; place in bowl.

▣ Peel celeriac and cut into 1-inch chunks. Place in saucepan, cover with water, and simmer 30 minutes, until knife can easily pierce to center. Drain.

▣ Place cod in food processor, add garlic, and pulse to finely chop. With machine running, slowly pour in oil through feed tube; process until blended, stopping to scrape bowl with plastic spatula. Add warm celeriac; pulse until evenly smooth, not pureed. Add 1/2 cup cream and the pepper; pulse to blend—the mixture should have a little texture. (Add a little more cream if needed.) Scrape into 1 1/2-quart gratin dish. Cover; and refrigerate up to 3 days before serving.

▣ To serve: Preheat oven to 425° F. Bake brandade 10 minutes, until hot and browned. Serve with endive for dipping.

Per serving: 249 calories, 9 g carbohydrates, 30 g protein, 10 g fat

Double-Salmon Rillettes

For a softer spread, use half crème fraîche (or sour cream) and half butter.

8 ounces fresh salmon fillet,
    skinned
1 cup dry white wine or red wine
4 ounces smoked salmon, diced
1/2 cup unsalted butter, softened
2 tablespoons minced shallot or
    chives

1 teaspoon grated peeled fresh
    ginger or more to taste
1/2 teaspoon grated lemon zest
1/4 teaspoon Chinese five-spice
    powder
fine sea salt to taste
cucumber slices for serving

▪ Combine fresh salmon and wine in medium skillet over medium heat; heat to boiling. Cover fish with waxed paper; cover pan with lid. Reduce heat to medium-low; cook 5 minutes or until fish is barely cooked through. Place fish in medium bowl to cool.

▪ Separate cooked salmon into big flakes with a fork. Add smoked salmon, butter, shallots, and seasonings; mix gently. Taste and adjust seasoning if necessary. Spoon into a shallow bowl or crock. Cover; refrigerate at least 1 hour to allow flavors to marry. Serve on cucumber slices.

Per serving: 184 calories, trace carbohydrates, 4 g protein, 7 g fat

Greek-Style Mussels in Garlic-Goat Cheese Broth

MAKES 4 SERVINGS

If you are craving mussels, this dish is for you.

**3 cups Court Bouillon,
    (see page 91)**
**2 garlic cloves, crushed through a
    press**
2 teaspoons grated lemon zest

2 pounds mussels, scrubbed
3/4 cup crumbled feta cheese
**1/2 cup lightly packed fresh
    parsley leaves**

Heat Court Bouillon, garlic, and lemon zest in large skillet to boiling over high heat; add mussels and cover. Cook, shaking pan to mix, 1 minute. Sprinkle cheese and parsley over mussels, cover, and steam 1 to 2 minutes, until mussels open, shaking pan to distribute the ingredients evenly and to give the mussels room to open. Discard any unopened mussels. Serve in bowls, with empty bowls for the shells.

Per serving: 158 calories, 5 g carbohydrates, 16 g protein, 8 g fat

Frida's Guacamole with Chipotle Chiles

MAKES 8 SERVINGS

If I have the luxury of a planned last meal on earth, it would begin with margaritas and this guacamole (and thick corn tortillas!).

4 ripe but firm Haas avocados, peeled and pitted
1/2 medium onion, chopped
1 large tomato, peeled, seed, and chopped
1/4 cup finely chopped fresh cilantro
4 canned chipotle chiles in adobo sauce, chopped
fine sea salt to taste

Crush avocados in large bowl with potato masher to desired coarseness. Stir in remaining ingredients; toss gently to mix.

Per serving: 137 calories, 9 g carbohydrates, 2 g protein, 12 g fat

Sautéed Oysters on Spinach Beds

MAKES 8 SERVINGS

Oysters are higher in carbs than most shellfish, so portion control must be practiced!

1/2 cup butter plus extra for greasing ramekins
3 paper-thin slices Serrano or prosciutto ham, finely chopped
1/3 cup finely chopped shallots
1/2 jalapeño, finely diced
1 pint shucked oysters, drained
1 tablespoon grated lemon zest

Tabasco sauce to taste
fine sea salt to taste
freshly ground pepper to taste
finely chopped fresh parsley for garnish
Steakhouse Creamed Spinach, hot, (see page 182)

■ Butter 8 (6-ounce) ramekins. Melt butter in large heavy skillet over medium heat, add ham, and sauté 2 minutes, until slightly crisp. Add shallots and jalapeño; cook 2 minutes. Add oysters; cook until plumped and beginning to curl on the edges. Stir in lemon zest; season with Tabasco, salt, and pepper.

■ Divide spinach among ramekins; spoon oyster mixture on top, dividing evenly. Sprinkle with parsley and serve immediately.

Per serving: 241 calories, 5 g carbohydrates, 6 g protein, 23 g fat

Party Pickled Shrimp

You can make a seafood mix to include cooked bay or sea scallops, halved lengthwise, and cooked squid, cut into rings, for part of the shrimp.

2 pounds shrimp, cooked shelled, and deveined

2 small (1-inch diameter) red onions, peeled, very thinly sliced

2 lemons, very thinly sliced

2 celery stalks, sliced on the diagonal into 1/2 inch thick pieces

1/2 cup sliced black olives or sliced pimiento-stuffed green olives or 1/4 cup each

2 bay leaves, crushed

1 (16-ounce) bottle Italian dressing

1/4 cup white vinegar

1/2 teaspoon Tabasco sauce or to taste

1/4 teaspoon salt or to taste

1/4 cup chopped fresh parsley

▓ Layer shrimp, onions, lemon slices, celery, and olives in a large glass serving bowl, repeating layers until all the ingredients are used.

▓ Combine dressing, vinegar, bay leaves, Tabasco sauce, and salt in a bowl and whisk until thick and smooth. Pour over shrimp mixture. Cover and refrigerate 24 hours.

▓ Before serving, add parsley and toss well to mix ingredients and coat with dressing. Adjust seasonings to taste. Use a slotted spoon to serve.

Per serving: 225 calories, 6 g carbohydrates, 24 g protein, 12 g fat

Hot Crab and Water Chestnut Dip

MAKES 8 SERVINGS

This can easily be transformed into a cold dip by leaving out the cream cheese.

1 (8-ounce) package cream cheese, softened

1 (8-ounce) container sour cream

2 tablespoons roasted garlic, (see page 100)

soy or teriyaki sauce

1 tablespoon grated fresh ginger

1 teaspoon fresh lemon juice

1/4 teaspoon salt

1/8 teaspoon coarsely ground black pepper

1 pound fresh lump crabmeat

1 (8-ounce) can water chestnuts, drained, finely chopped

2 tablespoons rice wine or dry sherry

Cream or milk for thinning, if necessary

Wide celery sticks for dipping

▓ Combine cream cheese, sour cream, garlic, soy sauce, lemon juice, ginger, salt, and pepper in the top of a double boiler placed over simmering water. Heat through, stirring often.

▓ When cheese has melted, add crabmeat, water chestnuts, and sherry. Add cream to reach desired consistency. Serve in a chafing dish or fondue pot with celery for dipping.

Per serving: 243 calories, 9 g carbohydrates, 14 g protein, 16 g fat

Clams Casino

Everyone has a different but equally delicious recipe for these tasty bites. My secret weapon is the applewood-smoked bacon!

1 dozen small cherrystone or large littleneck clams, purged (see Note)

1 tablespoon cornmeal

3 strips applewood-smoked bacon

1/4 cup chopped jarred, canned, or homemade roasted red peppers

1/4 cup grated Vidalia or other sweet onion

2 tablespoons butter, softened

2 tablespoons chopped fresh parsley

2 tablespoons fresh lemon juice or to taste

1 tablespoon roasted garlic soy or teriyaki sauce

■ Open clams carefully over a bowl to catch juices. Remove and discard halves of the clamshells without the clams. Place shell with clam on baking sheet; loosen clams slightly to make eating easier.

■ Cut each bacon slice into 4 equal pieces. Place in skillet over medium heat; fry just until fat starts to render. Remove to plate.

■ Combine peppers, onion, butter, parsley, lemon juice, garlic and soy sauce in a bowl; mix well. Stir in some reserved clam juice to make a moist mixture; spoon on top of clams, dividing evenly. Place a strip of bacon on each (clams can be made ahead to this point, covered, and refrigerated up to 4 hours.) When ready to cook clams, preheat broiler. Broil about 4 inches from heat 3 to 4 minutes, until bacon is crisp and clams are steaming.

Note: Before using clams, cover with cold water in bowl, sprinkle with 1 tablespoon cornmeal, and let stand 30 minutes to purge of sand. Drain and rinse.

Per serving: 192 calories, 5 g carbohydrates, 8 g protein, 16 g fat

Pork Tenderloin With Mustard Sauce and Sesame Seeds

MAKES 12 SERVINGS

The mustard dipping sauce has some kick to it, but you can tame the heat by thinning it with water to a glaze-like consistency.

1 (1-pound) pork tenderloins, trimmed of silverskin and fat

1/4 cup hoisin sauce

1 teaspoon garlic powder

1/2 cup Spicy Mustard Dipping Sauce, (see page 80)

1/2 cup toasted sesame seeds

▦ Preheat oven to 400° F. Line small roasting pan with foil. Place pork in pan, rub with hoisin, and sprinkle with garlic powder. Roast 20 minutes, until instant-read thermometer inserted in center reads 145° F to 150° F. Cover loosely with foil; cool 10 minutes.

▦ Thinly slice pork; place on a platter. Place sauce and seeds in separate small bowls next to the pork. To eat, lightly dip a slice of pork in sauce and then seeds.

Per serving: 154 calories, 5 g carbohydrates, 10 g protein, 11 g fat

Zucchini-Stuffed Mushrooms

MAKES 18 SERVINGS

You can vary the cheese and herb mix as you wish. Gruyère is nice with thyme; Gorgonzola, with chopped fennel seeds.

18 large mushrooms, cleaned and trimmed

1½ tablespoon extra-virgin olive oil, divided, plus more for greasing dish

1 tablespoon dry white wine

1 large garlic clove, crushed through a press

1 medium zucchini (8 ounces), finely chopped

¼ cup grated Asiago or Provolone cheese

salt, freshly ground pepper, and dried oregano leaves to taste

■ Preheat oven to 375° F. Grease a shallow 2-quart baking dish with oil.

■ Remove mushroom stems; finely chop. Heat 1 tablespoon oil in large skillet over medium heat; add mushroom caps; sauté 3 minutes. Add wine and sauté 3 minutes, until caps start to soften but are still firm in center. Place caps stem side up in baking dish.

■ Heat remaining oil in skillet, add garlic, and sauté 30 seconds. Add mushroom stems and zucchini and sauté 3 minutes, until crisp-tender. Remove from heat; stir in cheese and seasonings to taste. Spoon mixture into caps, dividing evenly. Bake 20 minutes, until cheese melts.

Per serving: 24 calories, 1 g carbohydrates, 1 g protein, 2 g fat

Roasted Eggplant and Mushroom Dip

MAKES 12 SERVINGS

This mixture will fill 24 small sautéed mushroom caps. Bake 20 minutes at 375° F.

1 medium eggplant (1¼ pounds)
2 tablespoons extra-virgin olive
   oil plus extra for greasing pan
1 to 2 large garlic cloves, crushed
   through a garlic press
2 tablespoons fresh lemon juice
   or to taste
4 ounces mushrooms, cleaned
   and quartered
½ cup chopped pitted black
   oil-cured olives

3 tablespoons chopped fresh
   parsley, oregano, or basil
¼ teaspoon ground cumin or to
   taste
salt and freshly ground pepper
   to taste
yellow squash, zucchini, and bell
   pepper strips for dipping

▓ Preheat oven to 450° F. Line a small roasting pan with foil; oil foil. Halve eggplant lengthwise; score flesh sides twice, being careful not to cut through skin. Place flesh side down in pan. Roast 45 minutes, until completely soft. Cool completely.

▓ Scoop eggplant flesh into food processor. Add garlic and 1 tablespoon lemon juice; puree. Heat oil in large skillet over medium heat. Add mushrooms and sauté 3 minutes, until tender. Add 1 tablespoon lemon juice; sauté 3 minutes. Add eggplant puree; sauté 3 minutes. Remove from heat; stir in olives, parsley, cumin, salt, and pepper. Taste and adjust seasonings.

Per serving: 42 calories, 4 g carbohydrates, 1 g protein, 3 g fat

Drunken Chicken Bites

MAKES 8 SERVINGS

Most of the work on these classic Chinese appetizers is done a day ahead of serving.

2 celery stalks, cut into 2-inch pieces

6 fat green onions, white portion cut into 2-inch pieces plus 1/4 cup chopped green tops for serving

1-inch piece peeled fresh ginger, sliced

1 teaspoon salt

1/4 teaspoon white pepper

2 cups water

6 boneless, skinless chicken breasts (about 3 pounds total), tenderloins removed for another use

1/2 cup rice wine or dry sherry

3 tablespoons soy sauce

1 tablespoon dark sesame oil

2 tablespoons green-onion tops

2 tablespoons toasted sesame seeds

■ Heat celery, green onions, ginger, salt, pepper, and water in deep skillet over medium heat to boiling. Simmer 5 minutes. Add chicken; cover. Heat to simmering; remove from heat. Let stand 20 minutes. With tongs, transfer chicken to shallow dish so breasts are in one layer. Add wine, cover, and refrigerate overnight, turning breasts as regularly as you can manage.

■ To serve: Remove breasts to cutting board and cut into 1-inch chunks. Place in a bowl and toss with soy sauce, sesame oil, and green-onion tops. Spoon out onto a serving platter using a slotted spoon and sprinkle with sesame seeds. Serve with toothpicks.

Per serving: 154 calories, 3.4 carbohydrates, 2 g protein, 4 g fat

Buffalo Chicken Wings

There doesn't seem to be a bad version of these in existence. These are nice and spicy and beautifully glazed. The dipping sauce is the best!

12 chicken wings (about 2 pounds)
3 tablespoons Louisiana hot
  sauce
2 tablespoons olive oil
1/4 cup Cajun Spice Rub,
  (see page 98)

1 cup Blue Cheese Dressing,
  (see page 77)
4 large celery stalks, trimmed,
  cut into 3-inch lengths.

■ Preheat oven to 400° F. Line large roasting pan with heavy-duty aluminum foil. Cut through wings at joints; discard wing tips. Place wings in prepared pan. Add 2 tablespoons hot sauce and the oil; toss to coat. Sprinkle with spice rub; toss to mix well.

■ Spread wings in single layer. Roast 30 minutes; turn wings. Roast 15 to 20 minutes, until cooked through.

■ Preheat broiler. Line baking sheet with heavy-duty foil. Using tongs, lift flat portion of wings from roasting pan and arrange on prepared baking sheet. Drizzle with half the remaining hot sauce; toss to coat. Broil until browned and crisp, turning once. Remove to serving dish. Repeat with drumstick portions. Serve with dressing and celery.

Note: Wings can marinate in sauce and spice rub in a zip-top plastic food storage bag in refrigerator up to 1 day in advance of cooking.

Per serving: 382 calories, 7 g carbohydrates, 21 g protein, 30 g fat

Chopped Chicken Liver

MAKES 32 SERVINGS IF SPREAD ON VEGETABLES

Although traditionally served on matzo, this is a tasty spread on juicy, crisp celery and radishes. Sprinkle with chopped fresh parsley and additional chopped egg before serving.

1 pound fresh chicken livers
2 tablespoons vegetable oil or
   schmaltz (rendered chicken fat)
2 tablespoons vegetable
   shortening
4 cups chopped onions

3 large hard-cooked eggs, mashed
   with a fork
kosher salt and freshly ground
   pepper to taste
sliced vegetables for serving

▨ Drain and rinse livers. Heat oil in large skillet over medium-high heat; sauté livers 3 minutes, until firm and slightly pink in center. (Do not overcook.) Remove with slotted spoon to plate; cool.

▨ Clean skillet; melt shortening over medium heat. Add onions; sauté 30 to 40 minutes, until caramelized, reducing heat as onions soften.

▨ Coarsely chop livers in food processor or by hand; place in bowl. Add onions and eggs; mix, gently adding enough onion cooking juices to moisten mixture. Season to taste. Cover; refrigerate at least 2 hours. Let sit at room temperature 15 minutes before serving.

Note: Make just a half-batch if you don't think you'll eat it all up within 3 days.

Per serving: 50 calories, 3 g carbohydrates, 3.5 g protein, 3 g fat

Salads

Frisée and Gorgonzola Salad

MAKES 4 SERVINGS

The bracing, salty nuggets of Italy's famous blue cheese dance in this mixture of tangy lettuce, juicy tomatoes, and crunchy pine nuts.

2 small bunches frisée or curly endive, broken into bite-size pieces
1/2 pint grape tomatoes, halved
1/4 cup crumbled Gorgonzola cheese

1/4 cup loosely packed Italian parsley leaves
1/4 cup Dijon Vinaigrette, (see page 76)
2 tablespoons toasted pine nuts

Place frisée in salad bowl; sprinkle tomatoes, cheese, and parsley on top. Drizzle with vinaigrette; toss to coat. Place on plates; sprinkle with pine nuts.

Per serving: 86 calories, 4 g carbohydrate, 3 g protein, 7 g fat

(See overleaf for recipe photo)

Mixed Greens and More Salad

A brief soaking in ice water reduces the intensity of the flavor and aroma of raw onions.

1 head Boston lettuce
3 bunches arugula
1 bunch watercress
3 cups spinach
1 small red onion
1 small red bell pepper, sliced
   into rings

1 small yellow bell pepper, sliced
   into rings
1/2 cup sliced pitted ripe olives
Shallot-Thyme Vinaigrette,
   (see page 76)

Rinse and spin dry greens; trim large stems from watercress and spinach. Place in salad bowl; chill 20 minutes, until crisp.

Meanwhile, cut onion crosswise into very thin rings. Soak in ice water 20 minutes; drain and pat dry with paper towels.

Place peppers and olives on greens; pour half the dressing over mixture. Toss to coat, adding more dressing as needed.

Each of 12 servings: 114 calories, 4 g carbohydrate, 1 g protein, 13 g fat

Escarole, Radicchio, and Belgian Endive Salad

MAKES 4 TO 6 SERVINGS

A trio of bitter but beautiful lettuces is the perfect match for the Hot Brie Dressing.

1/2 **small head escarole (8 ounces), rinsed**
1 **small head radicchio**

1 **small head Belgian endive**
Hot Brie Dressing with Mixed Fresh Herbs, (see page 79)

■ Tear escarole and radicchio into bite-size pieces; place in salad bowl. Cut endive crosswise into thick rings; add to greens. Add dressing; toss to coat. Serve at once.

Each of 6 servings: 165 calories, 4 g carbohydrate, 5 g protein, 15 g fat

BLT Salad

The flavors of the perfect sandwich are here in breadless form.

8 cups torn romaine lettuce leaves
1/4 pound slab bacon, cut in
  1/2-inch dice
1 tablespoon olive oil
1 pint cherry tomatoes, halved

1 clove garlic, crushed through
  a press
1/2 teaspoon freshly ground pepper
2 tablespoons red-wine vinegar

▪ Place lettuce in salad bowl. Cook bacon in large skillet until crisp; remove to bowl. Discard all but 1 tablespoon fat from pan. Add olive oil; heat over medium-high heat. Add tomatoes; sauté 1 minute. Add garlic and pepper; sauté 30 seconds. Add vinegar; stir to coat. Pour over lettuce; toss to coat.

Per serving: 200 calories, 6 g carbohydrate, 8 g protein, 17 g fat

Vegetable Salad Niçoise

MAKES 4 SERVINGS

For a more substantial salad, sprinkle 2 cups diced firm tofu or diced, cooked chicken and a couple of chopped hard-cooked eggs over the bottom of the dish before adding the vegetables. For anchovyphobes, use julienned carrots or red and/or green bell peppers to make the lattice.

1/2 **pound green beans, trimmed, cooked, cooled**

1 **English cucumber, peeled, thinly sliced crosswise**

1 **cup cherry tomatoes, halved**

1 **(2-ounce) jar anchovy fillets, drained, sliced lengthwise into long slivers**

32 **halves pitted, oil-cured black olives**

1/4 **cup Dijon Vinaigrette, (see page 76)**

In shallow serving dish, place green beans. Cover with a thin layer of cucumber. Make a lattice of anchovies on top, and fill in each space with an olive half. Arrange tomatoes around edge. Sprinkle with dressing and serve.

Per serving: 67 calories, 6 g carbohydrate, 3 g protein, 4 g fat

Chinese Broccoli Salad

MAKES 6 SERVINGS

Here's a use for those broccoli stalks, once you've whacked off the florets.

2 bunches broccoli stems or
    1 bunch broccoli
2 teaspoons salt

Dressing
3 tablespoons soy sauce
2 tablespoons dark sesame oil
1 tablespoon distilled white
    vinegar or rice vinegar
pinch of sugar

■ Peel broccoli stems with a paring knife and cut into 1-inch diagonal pieces through the stalk, turning the stalk a quarter turn with every slice. If using whole stalks, trim off florets first. Cut big florets into pieces the size of the cut stalks.

■ Cook broccoli 5 minutes in saucepan of boiling, salted water, until crisp-tender. Drain; place in a bowl. Set aside to cool.

■ Combine dressing ingredients in a small bowl; whisk to blend. Just before serving, pour dressing over broccoli; toss to coat.

Per serving: 78 calories, 7 g carbohydrate, 4 g protein, 5 g fat

Cucumber, Carrot, and Cellophane Noodle Salad

MAKES 8 SERVINGS

You can find the thin bean-paste noodles in Asian grocery stores.

2 ounces cellophane noodles
2 medium carrots, peeled and cut
   into 3-inch x ⅛-inch julienne
1 English cucumber, peeled,
   quartered, seeded, and cut
   into 3-inch x ⅛-inch julienne
2 large green onions, trimmed
   and cut into 3-inch x ⅛-inch
   julienne

3 cloves garlic, minced
2 teaspoons salt, divided
½ teaspoon Szechuan or pink
   peppercorns
2 tablespoons soy sauce
1 tablespoon hot chili oil
1 tablespoon dark sesame oil
1 tablespoon rice wine vinegar

▓ Place noodles in a large bowl; cover with boiling water. Soak 10 minutes.

▓ Meanwhile, combine carrots, cucumber, green onions, and garlic in a bowl and toss with 1 teaspoon salt. Set aside.

▓ Heat peppercorns in small skillet over medium heat until fragrant. Place in glass or metal bowl; crush with the end of a rolling spoon or back of a spoon. Add remaining ingredients and 1 teaspoon salt; whisk to combine.

▓ Drain noodles; cut into 3-inch pieces with kitchen shears. (Pieces don't have to be exact.) Place in a bowl. Rinse cucumber mixture; pat dry with a clean kitchen towel. Add to noodles. Add dressing; toss to coat.

Per serving: 70 calories, 9 g carbohydrate, 3 g protein, 4 g fat

Fresh Tofu (Bean Curd) Salad

The rich, flavorful dressing and bright, juicy green onions give the nutritious but bland tofu some personality.

4 (3-inch) squares or 1 pound
   fresh firm tofu, drained and
   patted dry
1/2 cup chopped green onion,
   green part only

Dressing
3 tablespoons soy sauce
3 tablespoons dark sesame oil
2 teaspoons grated peeled fresh
   ginger
pinch of sugar

▓ Cut bean curd into 1/2-inch dice and place in a medium bowl. Add green onions.

▓ Combine dressing ingredients in a small bowl and whisk to blend. Just before serving, pour dressing over tofu and toss to coat.

Per serving: 128 calories, 4 g carbohydrate, 7 g protein, 10 g fat

Kim Chee (Korean Pickled Cabbage)

MAKES 8 SERVINGS

The national dish of its native land, this spicy mixture is eaten at every meal. I like to serve it with grilled meat dishes that have been marinated containing dark sesame-oil.

3 cups shredded inner leaves
  Napa cabbage
2 tablespoons salt
3 green onions, cut into 1 1/2-inch
  pieces
3 to 4 large garlic cloves, crushed
  through a garlic press

1 1/2 to 2 teaspoons coarse Korean
  or other chili powder or
  Tabasco or other hot pepper
  sauce
1 teaspoon grated peeled fresh
  ginger
water

▨ Place cabbage in nonreactive bowl, sprinkle with 1 tablespoon salt; toss to coat. Let stand 30 minutes. Drain; squeeze gently to extract excess moisture.

▨ Rinse cabbage; place in nonreactive bowl. Add green onions, garlic, pepper sauce, ginger, and remaining 1 tablespoons salt; toss to coat. Add cold water to cover. Cover with plastic wrap; let mixture stand at room temperature 1 to 5 days, stirring occasionally. Drain and transfer to a jar. Cover tightly and store in refrigerator. Serve at room temperature or slightly chilled.

Per serving: 12 calories, 3 g carbohydrate, trace protein, trace fat

Red Cabbage and Blue Cheese Slaw

MAKES 12 SERVINGS

The generous ratio of cheesy dressing to cabbage is only one reason this salad is great. Parsley and lemon add a spirited lift of fresh flavor.

1/2 (1-pound) head red cabbage
1/2 (1-pound) head green cabbage
1 cup finely chopped fresh
   parsley (about 2 bunches)

2 1/2 cups Blue Cheese Dressing,
   (see page 77)
1/4 cup grainy mustard
1 tablespoon grated lemon zest

■ Remove a few outer leaves of the cabbages, rinse, dry and use to line a large serving bowl. Quarter and core cabbages; cut wedges crosswise into thin shreds. Place in a large bowl with 3/4 cup parsley.

■ Combine dressing and mustard in a medium bowl and whisk until blended. Pour into cabbage mixture and toss to coat. Sprinkle with remaining parsley. Cover and refrigerate at least 2 hours before serving.

166 calories, 10 g carbohydrate, 4 g protein, 12 g fat

Mary Gallagher's Coleslaw

MAKES 8 SERVINGS

My sister-in-law Mary is one of the best cooks I know. She's skilled, organized, and has a great palate for everyday foods as well as show-stopping menus. Ever since she served this at one of our family reunion Thanksgiving dinners, I can't have turkey without it!

1 (1-pound) head green cabbage, cored and grated or chopped

2 tablespoons chopped green bell pepper (or 1 tablespoon each chopped green and red bell pepper)

2 tablespoons finely chopped fresh parsley

1/2 cup distilled white vinegar

2 teaspoons dry mustard

1 1/2 cups mayonnaise

salt, pepper, and garlic salt to taste

■ Combine cabbage, bell pepper and parsley in a large bowl. Heat vinegar and mustard to boiling in a small saucepan and pour over the cabbage mixture. Toss to coat and let stand about 5 minutes.

■ Add mayonnaise and mix well. Season with salt, pepper, and garlic salt.

Per serving: 125 calories, 9 g carbohydrate, 1 g protein, 10 g fat

Slivered Cucumber and Chicken Salad

MAKES 2 SERVINGS

Because of the simplicity of the salad, it is important to have juicy chicken. I like to poach the breast most of the way and let it finish cooking in its poaching liquid.

3 to 4 Kirby cucumbers, peeled
    and julienned
1 large cooked chicken breast
    half, skinned, boned, and
    julienned

Dressing
2 tablespoons rice vinegar
1 tablespoon soy sauce
1/2 teaspoon dry yellow mustard
    or dry wasabi
1/2 teaspoon salt

1 teaspoon toasted sesame seeds
    for serving

■ Combine cucumbers and chicken in a bowl. Mix dressing ingredients in a cup and drizzle on top. Toss to coat. Cover and marinate in refrigerator 30 minutes to 1 hour. Serve cold, sprinkled with sesame seeds.

Per serving: 150 calories, 4 g carbohydrate, 28 g protein, 2 g fat

Grilled Fennel Salad with Shaved Parmesan

MAKES 4 SERVINGS

This simple mix showcases the anise flavor and juicy, crunchy texture of fennel.

2 (8-ounce) bulbs fennel
6 tablespoons best-quality
    extra-virgin olive oil
fine sea salt to taste
1/4 cup fresh parsley leaves

1/4 cup shaved Parmesan cheese
3 tablespoons fresh lemon juice
2 tablespoons Parsley Oil,
    (see page 74)

■ Preheat griddle over medium-low heat until hot. Cut off both ends of each fennel bulb so you can see the separate rings. Cut bulbs crosswise into 3/4-inch slices, keeping the rings intact. Brush cut sides with 4 tablespoons oil; sprinkle lightly with salt. Grill slices about 4 minutes per side, until crisp-tender and caramelized, basting with 2 tablespoons oil. Remove fennel to plate to cool.

■ To serve: Keep fennel slices intact until placed on plates; artistically release the rings so they fall out of place but stack on each other. Sprinkle with parsley, then Parmesan. Drizzle lemon juice and Parsley Oil over all.

289 calories, 10 g carbohydrate, 4 g protein, 28 g fat

Curly Celery Salad with Mustard Dressing

MAKES 6 SERVINGS

You can use light cream instead of sour cream for a saucier dressing.

**4 bunches celery (don't panic;
only inner yellow portions
will be used!)**
1 cup cherry tomatoes, quartered
1/4 cup chopped fresh parsley
**3 to 4 tablespoons fresh lemon
juice**

**1 tablespoon German mustard or
other hot mustard or to taste**
1/2 teaspoon salt or to taste
**1/4 teaspoon freshly ground
pepper to taste**
3/4 cup sour cream

■ Use outer celery ribs for something else; trim inner tender ribs of any dark portions but keep leaves on. Cut ribs lengthwise into 1/8- to 1/4-inch strips; cut crosswise into 2-inch lengths. Place in large pot of ice water several hours, until curled, adding ice as it melts.

■ Drain celery; dry in salad spinner, in batches, if necessary. Pile into large chilled bowl; add tomatoes and parsley. Place 3 tablespoons lemon juice, the mustard, 1/2 teaspoon salt, and 1/4 teaspoon pepper in jar with tight-fitting lid; shake to combine. Add sour cream; shake to combine. Taste; adjust seasonings. Pour over celery; toss to coat. Serve chilled.

Per serving: 72 calories, 6 g carbohydrate, 2 g protein, 5 g fat

Celeriac Rémoulade

MAKES 8 SERVINGS AS A SIDE SALAD (6 SERVINGS AS A FIRST COURSE)

As much as I love this salad, it requires patience and determination to sliver the hard bulb by hand. (It's too hard to cut strips with a processor and I don't like the salad with grated or shredded pieces.) Thinly slicing the bulb first and then stacking and slicing a few of the layers at a time is the most efficient way I know. You can buy jarred, pre-sliced celeriac if you don't want to fuss, but try it at least once with fresh.

1 large bulb celeriac (about 1¹/₂ pounds)

1 tablespoon fresh lemon juice

1 small carrot, peeled, julienned (optional)

³/₄ cup Rémoulade Sauce, and more if needed, (see page 81)

salt and freshly ground pepper to taste

1 to 2 tablespoons chopped fresh parsley

▓ Peel the bulb with a paring knife; cut it in half through the top and root using a cleaver or chef's knife, and place bulbs flat sides down on a cutting board. Cut each into ¹/₄ inch thick slices; turn slices and stack in 2 piles. Cut each stack into ¹/₄ inch thick slices. Place in a medium bowl; toss with lemon juice to keep from browning.

▓ Add carrot and Rémoulade Sauce; toss to coat. Taste and add more sauce if needed. Adjust seasoning if necessary. Sprinkle with parsley. Serve chilled.

Per serving: 189 calories, 9 g carbohydrate, 1 g protein, 17 g fat

Soups

Fish, Peanut, and Coconut-Milk Soup

MAKES 6 SERVINGS

This is a traditional breakfast soup of Cambodia and Laos. Here chunks of hearty catfish control the pot.

Peanut Sauce:

- 2 tablespoons peanut oil or vegetable oil
- 4-inch piece fresh lemongrass, thinly sliced
- 3 hot red chilies, chopped
- 3 (double) fresh kaffir lime leaves, stem and main vein removed, finely chopped
- 3 green onions, finely chopped
- 1/2 cup crushed fresh raw peanuts
- 6 large garlic cloves, peeled and finely chopped
- 1 can (about 14 ounces) unsweetened coconut milk

- 1 quart water
- 2 tablespoons fresh lime juice
- 2 (1/4 inch thick) slices peeled galangal (fresh or frozen), optional
- 1 1/2 pounds skinless catfish or other firm, flavorful fillets, cut into 2-inch strips
- 6 tablespoons Thai or Vietnamese fish sauce
- 1/4 cup fresh cilantro leaves
- 2 tablespoons finely chopped fresh basil leaves

▓ Heat oil in large nonstick skillet over medium heat. Add lemongrass, garlic, chilies, lime leaves, green onions, and peanuts; sauté over medium-high heat 3 to 5 minutes, until peanuts are browned. Add garlic; sauté 1 minute, until tender. Add coconut milk; heat to simmering. Keep warm.

▓ Combine water, lime juice, and galangal in 3-quart saucepan; heat to simmering. Stir in fish; simmer gently 2 minutes, until fish separates when poked with fork. Stir in fish sauce, cilantro, and basil; simmer 2 minutes.

Per serving: 344 calories, 8 g carbohydrate, 23 g protein, 25 g fat

(See overleaf for recipe photo)

Oyster Stew

Have soup bowls heated before you start to make the soup. Even though it uses 3 pans, this is about as quick a recipe as you can find and it is simply delicious.

2 cups milk
2 cups light cream or half-and-half
1 quart shucked oysters and their liquor
2 tablespoons butter

salt and freshly ground white pepper to taste
celery salt to taste
sweet Spanish or Hungarian paprika

▓ Combine milk and cream in a medium saucepan over medium heat and heat until small bubbles form around the edge of the pan. Keep warm.

▓ Drain oyster liquor into another medium saucepan over medium-high heat; heat to boiling. Pour all but 2 tablespoons liquor into milk mixture. Add oysters and butter to reserved liquor; heat over medium heat until edges of oysters start to curl. Immediately pour oysters and liquid into hot milk mixture; season with salt, pepper, and celery salt. Ladle into bowls and dust with paprika.

Per serving: 273 calories, 10 g carbohydrate, 8 g protein, 23 g fat

Cream of Lettuce Soup

The first sips will elicit surprise "oohs and aahs" from the table, no matter how delicate the green used; even the much-maligned Iceberg will shine! Try it with watercress—for a hot or cold peppery palate pleaser.

2 tablespoons butter	1/2 cup 2% milk
2 large heads lettuce, rinsed, shredded	1/2 cup crème fraiche
1 medium onion, thinly sliced	salt and freshly ground white pepper to taste
4 cups chicken broth	1/4 cup chopped fresh mint

▪ Melt butter in large saucepan over medium heat; add lettuce and onion. Cover and cook 5 minutes, until lettuce is translucent.

▪ Combine broth and milk and heat to boiling in small saucepan; pour into lettuce mixture. (Mixture will curdle if milk is added cold.) Simmer over low heat 20 minutes. Cool; carefully puree, in batches, in blender. Pour into cleaned saucepan.

▪ Combine 2% milk and crème fraîche in another medium saucepan (if serving hot) or bowl (if serving cold) and whisk to combine. Whisk in lettuce mixture until blended. Taste and season with salt and pepper. Heat until almost boiling if serving hot; ladle soup into bowls and sprinkle generously with mint.

Per serving: 142 calories, 9 g carbohydrate, 7 g protein, 9 g fat

Asian Crab Soup

MAKES 6 SERVINGS

2 tablespoons vegetable oil
4 green onions, trimmed and
   chopped
1 cup crabmeat
6 cups fish stock or chicken broth
2 tablespoons rice wine or dry
   sherry

1 teaspoon grated peeled fresh
   ginger
1/4 teaspoon freshly ground pepper
salt to taste
2 egg whites, slightly beaten
2 tablespoons minced ham
1 tablespoon chopped fresh
   cilantro

Heat oil in 3-quart saucepan and add green onions. Sauté 2 minutes, until softened and fragrant. Add crab, stock, wine, ginger, pepper, and salt. Heat to boiling. Gradually whisk in egg whites, using chopsticks to separate whites into strands as they cook. Heat 1 minute, until whites are firm but not tough. Serve in small bowls. Sprinkle each with a little bit of ham and cilantro.

Per serving: 188 calories, 3 g carbohydrate, 18 g protein, 11 g fat

Italian Egg-Ribbon Soup
(Stracciatella)

The Romans add shredded spinach to this otherwise plain but delicious soup.

2 cups seasoned chicken broth	2 eggs
1/2 clove garlic, crushed through a press	2 tablespoons freshly grated Parmesan cheese

▨ Heat broth with garlic in small saucepan over medium-high heat to simmering. Beat eggs with 2 tablespoons cheese in a bowl with a fork until blended and all the white has been mixed; slowly pour into soup, then stir quickly just until ribbons form. Sprinkle with additional cheese. Serve immediately.

Per serving: 193 calories, 1 g carbohydrate, 10 g protein, 5 g fat

Egg-Drop Soup

MAKES 4 SERVINGS

Bouillon cubes make a flavorful and quick broth, but you may need to use low-sodium soy sauce or 4 cubes to 6 cups water to obtain the optimum saltiness. Taste as you go.

1 tablespoon peanut oil or
    vegetable oil
1/2 cup finely chopped celery
1/4 cup finely chopped onion
6 cups chicken broth or vegetable
    stock
1 tablespoon soy sauce
2 teaspoons rice wine

1/4 teaspoon white pepper or
    more to taste
3 egg whites
2 green onions, minced
2 tablespoons mixed cilantro
    leaves and chopped roots
salt to taste if necessary

Heat oil in a 2-quart saucepan over medium heat and add celery and onion. Sauté 7 minutes, until tender. Add broth, soy sauce, wine, and pepper and heat to boiling. Simmer over low heat 10 minutes.

Lightly beat egg whites until frothy in a bowl with chopsticks and slowly pour into soup. Do not stir or the soup will get cloudy. Let stand 1 minute, until egg whites set. Add green onions and cilantro and heat through 1 minute. Taste and adjust seasoning if necessary. Ladle into bowls.

Per serving: 118 calories, 4.5 g carbohydrate, 11 g protein, 6 g fat

Chinese-Mushroom Soup

Substitute tofu for the pork and eliminate the ham, if you want a vegetarian soup.

12 medium dried black
   mushrooms
6 cups hot vegetable or meat
   stock or broth
1/2 pound shredded lean pork
   tenderloin
12 peeled fresh water chestnuts,
   sliced, or 2 (8-ounce) cans
   sliced water chestnuts, drained

1 (8-ounce can) bamboo shoots,
   drained
1 bunch baby spinach, rinsed well
2 ounces ham, julienned
2 tablespoons chopped green
   onions
2 teaspoons low-sodium soy sauce
1 teaspoon grated peeled fresh
   ginger

▓ Soak mushrooms in hot stock in a 3-quart saucepan until soft, about 15 minutes. Squeeze liquid from caps back into bowl of soaking liquid. Discard stems and thinly slice caps.

▓ Heat stock to boiling, add pork, and reduce heat to medium. Simmer pork 2 minutes, until tender. Add water chestnuts and bamboo shoots and simmer 20 minutes. Add spinach, ham, green onions, soy sauce, and ginger and simmer for 5 minutes.

Per serving: 186 calories, 10 g carbohydrate, 22 g protein, 7 g fat

Japanese Custard Soup
(Chawan-Mushi)

TV's "Iron Chef" fans know that the Japanese prize a food's texture as much as its flavor. This classic soup is on the cusp between a wet and set pudding.

vegetable oil for greasing custard cups	2 eggs
8 large shrimp, steamed, peeled, deveined; tails removed	2 cups chicken broth
	1/2 teaspoon salt
8 fresh spinach leaves, blanched	1/4 teaspoon white pepper
8 shiitake mushrooms, sliced	8 thin slices lemon for garnish
8 fresh, peeled or canned water chestnuts, sliced	low-sodium soy sauce for serving

▨ Prepare racks of bamboo steamers in a wok or metal steamer racks in a pot over 2 inches of steaming water.

▨ Grease 8 custard cups with oil. Place a shrimp, spinach leaf, sliced mushroom, and sliced water chestnut in each cup. In a 4-cup glass measure, beat eggs, salt, and pepper with a fork until eggs are broken and mixed. Stir in chicken broth. Pour custard into prepared cups.

▨ Arrange custard cups in a steamer and steam on medium heat 2 minutes. Reduce heat to low and steam 5 minutes. The soup should be firm but soft as custard. Serve drizzled with soy sauce and with lemon to twist.

Per serving: 80 calories, 9 g carbohydrate, 7 g protein, 2 g fat

Tomato and Okra Soup

The cinnamon adds a surprising, exotic touch to the simple ingredients.

8 ounces okra

1 tablespoon olive oil

1 onion, finely chopped

3 garlic cloves, crushed

1 (15-ounce) can chopped
   tomatoes

4 cups vegetable broth

2 (3-inch) cinnamon sticks

pinch of salt and pepper

▓ Cut off stem ends of okra pods; cut pots crosswise into 1/4-inch slices.

▓ Heat oil in a 2-quart saucepan over medium-high heat; sauté onion until 5 minutes, until it starts to brown. Add garlic; sauté 30 seconds, until fragrant. Stir in tomatoes and their juice and the broth. Heat to boiling; add okra and cinnamon sticks. Cook, 10 minutes, stirring occasionally, until okra is tender. Remove cinnamon sticks before serving.

Per serving: 60 calories, 9 g carbohydrate, 2 g protein, 3 g fat

Dressings
and Sauces

A Trio of Flavorful Herb Oils

Use these for flavoring while you lightly sauté or drizzle on for a concentrated herbal and color boost.

Parsley Oil:

Combine $1/2$ cup loosely packed Italian parsley leaves and $1/3$ cup olive oil in a blender and puree. Rinse $11/2$ teaspoons salt-packed capers and pat dry; add to puree and pulse to finely chop.

Makes about $2/3$ cup.

Per 2 teaspoon serving: 42 calories, trace carbohydrates, trace protein, 5 g fat

Dill Oil:

Blanch 1 bunch dill in saucepan of boiling water 1 minute, until wilted. Place in bowl of ice and water to cool thoroughly. Drain; squeeze out excess water. Puree in food processor or blender. With motor running, pour in $1/2$ cup olive oil in thin stream through opening in top of machine. Season with salt and freshly cracked pepper to taste. Make just before using, as it turns brown quickly.

Makes about 1 cup.

Per 2 teaspoon serving: 42 calories, trace carbohydrates, trace protein, 5 g fat

Basil Oil:

Blanch 8 ounces rinsed basil in saucepan of boiling water 1 minute, until wilted. Place in bowl of ice and water to cool thoroughly. Drain; squeeze out excess water. Puree in food processor or blender. With motor running, pour in 2 cups canola oil in thin stream through opening in top of machine.

Makes about $21/2$ cups.

Per 2 teaspoon serving: 42 calories, trace carbohydrates, trace protein, 5 g fat

(See overleaf for photo of recipes)

Crème Fraîche

MAKES 2 CUPS

Not always easy to find in grocery stores, this is an easy ingredient to make. You'll always have it on hand to use as a sour cream replacement and all-around prize recipe enhancer.

2 cups heavy cream
2 tablespoons buttermilk or sour
   cream

■ Heat heavy cream in small saucepan over low heat to 100F degrees. Whisk in buttermilk. Pour into a clean jar; cover. Let stand at room temperature 6 to 8 hours, until thickened. Refrigerate for 24 hours before using.

Per 1 tablespoon serving: 52 calories, 5 g carbohydrates, trace protein, 6 g fat

Dijon Vinaigrette

MAKES 12 SERVINGS

This is a tasty blend to use on salads and for marinading.

2 garlic cloves

1 cup loosely packed Italian
   parsley leaves

1/3 cup vegetable oil or olive oil

1/4 cup fresh lemon juice

1/4 cup red-wine vinegar

2 tablespoons Dijon mustard

1 teaspoon salt

1 teaspoon grated lemon zest

1/2 teaspoon freshly ground pepper

■ Mince garlic in food processor; add parsley and mince. Add remaining ingredients; process until smooth.

Per serving: 56 calories, 1 g carbohydrates, trace protein, 6 g fat

Shallot-Thyme Vinaigrette

MAKES 12 SERVINGS

The delicately garlic flavored, purple-tinted shallot makes this a bright dressing for green, meat, and vegetable salads.

2 large shallots, minced

2/3 cup olive oil

2 tablespoons fresh lemon juice

1 tablespoon white-wine vinegar

1 teaspoon minced fresh thyme
   leaves

1/2 teaspoon dry mustard

1/2 teaspoon salt

■ Place ingredients in jar with tight-fitting lid. Shake to blend.

Per serving: 114 calories, trace carbohydrates, trace protein, 12 g fat

Blue Cheese Dressing

MAKES 1 QUART

You can now call this classic and delicious blue cheese dressing recipe your very own.

2 cups mayonnaise

8 ounces Roquefort cheese, crumbled

6 ounces evaporated milk

1/4 cup fresh lemon juice

1 tablespoon chopped fresh parsley

2 tablespoons distilled white vinegar

1 teaspoon garlic salt

dash celery seed

■ Mix ingredients together in a bowl until blended.

Per ounce: 90 calories, 4 g carbohydrates, 2 g protein, 7 g fat

Green Tea Aioli

This spread is less garlicky than the classic French mayonaise so that you can enjoy the complexities of the green tea flavor.

1 large garlic clove, crushed
   through a garlic press
2 1/2 tablespoons fresh lemon juice
1 tablespoon Dijon mustard
1/2 teaspoon gyokuro (finest
   quality) green tea leaves, or
   more to taste

1 egg yolk
1/2 cup vegetable oil
4 anchovy fillets, minced
fine sea salt to taste
freshly ground white pepper
   to taste

■ Combine garlic, lemon juice, mustard, green tea, salt, and egg yolk in medium bowl; whisk until smooth. Add oil in a thin, steady stream while whisking until mixture emulsifies. Season with anchovies, salt, and pepper. Adjust green tea amount if desired.

Per tablespoon: 92 calories, 1 g carbohydrate, 4 g protein, 15 g fat

Hot Brie Dressing with Mixed Fresh Herbs

MAKES 1 CUP, 4 TO 6 SERVINGS

This creamy mix is especially nice with bitter greens like endive, radicchio, and escarole.

1/4 cup extra-virgin olive oil

1 large garlic clove, minced

1 1/2 teaspoons minced shallot
or green onion

1 1/2 teaspoons Dijon mustard

3/4 teaspoon chopped fresh chervil

1/2 teaspoon chopped fresh
tarragon leaves

1/4 cup balsamic vinegar

1 tablespoon fresh lemon juice

4 ounces Brie cheese, rind
removed, at room
temperature, cut into cubes

freshly ground pepper to taste

Heat oil in nonstick skillet over low heat, add garlic and shallot, and let infuse 15 minutes. Whisk in mustard, chervil, and tarragon until blended. Whisk in vinegar and lemon juice. Add cheese, a few pieces at a time, and whisk until melted and smooth. Use while hot.

3 tablespoon serving: 150 calories, 1 g carbohydrates, 4 g protein, 15 g fat

Spicy Mustard Dipping Sauce

MAKES ABOUT 1 1/2 CUPS

The mustard gets hotter the more you stir.

1/2 cup Chinese or English dry
   mustard
pinch of sugar or more to taste
water as needed

2 tablespoons rice vinegar
2 tablespoons fresh lemon juice
1/2 cup peanut oil
1 tablespoon dark sesame oil

In a medium bowl, whisk mustard with sugar and enough water to make a thin paste. Whisk in vinegar and lemon juice; gradually whisk in oils until an emulsion is formed. Taste; it may need a pinch or so more sugar. This sauce can be prepared a week or more ahead of serving.

Per tablespoon: 97 calories, 2 g carbohydrates, 1 g protein, 10 g fat

Rémoulade Sauce

This sauce will keep in the refrigerator up to 3 days. If it should separate in that time, allow it to come to room temperature and whisk the mixture with a fresh egg yolk in a clean bowl.

2 egg yolks
1 to 3 tablespoons fresh lemon juice
1 cup vegetable oil
1 tablespoon Dijon mustard or more to taste
1 anchovy, rinsed and chopped

1 tablespoon each, chopped fresh chervil, tarragon, parsley, and chives
1 teaspoon rinsed capers
1 teaspoon chopped cornichons
2 tablespoons olive oil
Salt and freshly ground white pepper to taste

■ Mix egg yolks and 1 tablespoon lemon juice in food processor until blended; with motor running, pour in enough vegetable oil to make a stiff paste. Add 1 tablespoon mustard; pulse to mix; add remaining vegetable oil.

■ Transfer mixture to a bowl; stir in anchovy, herbs, capers, and cornichon. Drizzle in olive oil while whisking. Taste; add salt and pepper. Adjust seasonings, making a pronounced mustard-flavored sauce.

Per tablespoon: 101 calories, trace carbohydrate, trace protein, 11 g fat

Sorrel Cream Sauce

MAKES 2 CUPS

The attractive sour flavor of sorrel combined with butter and cream create a luscious and tasty mix of simple ingredients. Serve it with fish, chicken, eggs, and in soups.

6 ounces sorrel leaves
1 cup beef, chicken, fish, or
    vegetable stock or broth
1/4 cup cream
2 tablespoons butter, softened

salt and freshly ground pepper
    to taste
1 tablespoon fresh lemon juice
    or to taste

◾ Rinse sorrel; with water still clinging to the leaves, place in a nonstick skillet. Cover; steam over medium-high heat 5 minutes, until very tender. Puree in food processor; press through a fine sieve into a bowl.

◾ Heat 3/4 cup stock or broth in 2-quart saucepan over medium-high heat until boiling; whisk in puree until smooth. Add cream and butter; whisk until butter melts. Whisk in more stock or broth if sauce is too thick for what you need it for. Season to taste with salt, pepper, and lemon juice.

Per 1/3 cup serving: 54 calories, 2 g carbohydrates, 1 g protein, 5 g fat

Feta Cream Sauce

MAKES ABOUT 3 CUPS

This is a tangy dipping sauce for anything with lamb, in particular. Try it with barbecued kebabs, grilled leg of lamb, even in lamb stews.

2 cups heavy cream
1 cup feta cheese, crumbled

salt and freshly ground white
pepper to taste

Place cream in a 3-quart saucepan and heat to boiling over medium heat. Simmer until cream is reduced to 1 cup. Add feta cheese and heat over medium-low until cheese melts. Whisk or buzz with a hand blender until sauce is smooth. Season to taste.

Per 1/4 cup serving: 85 calories, 2 g carbohydrate, 3 g protein, 7 g fat

Tomato Cream Sauce

MAKES 3 CUPS

This is a nice sauce for vegetables, pasta, and fish. You can stir in some shrimp or scallops, or a mixture of the two, and let them cook through, allowing their juices to flavor the mix.

2 tablespoons butter
1 large shallot, minced
1 1/2 cups heavy cream
1 cup tomato sauce (canned or
   homemade)
1 plum tomato, blanched, peeled,
   seeded, and cut lengthwise
   into 1/4-inch wide slices

1 tablespoon chopped fresh parsley
salt and freshly ground white
   pepper to taste

■   Melt butter in small saucepan over medium heat. Add shallot and sauté 5 minutes. Add cream; heat to boiling. Simmer 5 minutes, until slightly thickened. Stir in tomato sauce and tomato; heat until simmering. Stir in parsley and season with salt and pepper.

Per 1/2 cup serving: 130 calories, 7 g carbohydrates, 3 g protein, 11 g fat

Juniper Cream Sauce

This is a fragrant and delicious accompaniment to roasted, sautéed, or grilled veal, venison, rabbit, game birds, catfish, salmon, and ham. Oh yes, and grilled wild-boar sausages. If you can't find juniper berries, swirl a tablespoon of gin, or more to taste, into the finished sauce.

3 shallots, finely chopped
3 juniper berries, crushed
1 teaspoon dried thyme leaves
1/3 cup white-wine vinegar
1 cup beef stock
1 cup heavy cream
1/3 cup dry white wine

3 tablespoons unsalted butter,
    cut into bits
1 cup crème fraîche or sour
    cream, at room temperature
fine sea salt to taste
freshly ground white pepper
    to taste

■ Combine shallots, berries, thyme, and vinegar in a small saucepan and cook over medium heat until 1 tablespoon liquid remains. Add beef stock, cream, and wine; heat to boiling over medium-high heat, and simmer until reduced to 1 1/2 cups. Whisk in butter until melted. Whisk in crème fraîche until blended. Season with salt and pepper; keep warm until serving.

Per 1/4 cup serving: 140 calories, 3 g carbohydrates, 2 g protein, 13 g fat

Fresh Ginger Sauce

MAKES 1/2 CUP

This sauce is quite versatile; pour it on steamed fish fillets, chicken, or vegetables. Toss it with pasta or broiled, miso-glazed tofu. You can even use it on grilled fruit.

**2 tablespoons peanut or
  vegetable oil
2 tablespoons finely shredded,
  peeled fresh ginger**

**pinch of sugar
1/4 cup vegetable stock, chicken
  broth, white wine, or water
2 tablespoons light soy sauce**

■ Heat oil in a wok or small skillet. Add ginger and sugar; sauté 2 minutes, until fragrant. Add stock and soy sauce; heat to boiling. Simmer 2 minutes.

Per tablespoon: 65 calories, 1 g carbohydrates, trace protein, 7 g fat

Morel and Green-Peppercorn Sauce

MAKES 8 SERVINGS 2²/₃ CUPS

1 (3-ounce) package dried morels
1 cup warm water
2 tablespoons butter
1 tablespoon extra-virgin olive oil
1 shallot, minced
1 garlic clove, crushed through
   a press

1 tablespoons dried green
   peppercorns
2 tablespoons brandy or dry
   white vermouth
1 cup crème fraîche
sea salt
freshly ground pepper to taste

■ Place morels in a glass measuring cup. Add 1 cup very warm water and stir to mix. Let stand until morels are soft, about 15 minutes.

■ Melt butter in oil in small skillet or saucepan over medium heat. Add shallot and garlic and sauté 3 minutes, until tender. Stir in peppercorns and brandy. Add crème fraîche and whisk until blended. Strain morel soaking liquid into sauce and whisk until blended. Stir in morels and season to taste with pepper. Keep sauce warm over low heat until ready to serve.

Per serving: 106 calories, 2 g carbohydrates, trace protein, 10 g fat

Sour-Cream Horseradish Sauce

MAKES ABOUT 1 CUP

Here's a tangy topping for steaks of all kinds, from meat to seafood. It's really good as a cocktail sauce, replacing the ketchup-dominated dipping sauce we love for fried shrimp.

1 (8-ounce) container sour cream

dash of raspberry or balsamic
   vinegar

3 tablespoons grated fresh
   horseradish or more to taste

sea salt and freshly ground
   white pepper to taste

Combine sour cream, vinegar, horseradish, salt, and pepper in a medium bowl; stir to blend. Taste and adjust seasonings if necessary.

Per tablespoon: 27 calories, 1 g carbohydrates, trace protein, 2.5 g fat

Sour-Cream Tartar Sauce

MAKES ABOUT 1 CUP, 4 SERVINGS

Here's a flavorful coating for chilled cooked shellfish and salmon. It's less sweet than regular tartar sauce and has a bit of dill for an interesting twist.

3/4 cup sour cream
1 tablespoon mayonnaise
1 teaspoon minced fresh dill
2 teaspoons fresh lemon juice

pinch of dry mustard
fine sea salt to taste
freshly ground white pepper
   to taste

▢ Combine ingredients in a small bowl and whisk to combine. Chill before serving.

Per 1/4 cup serving: 92 calories, 2.6 g carbohydrates, 1 g protein, 9 g fat

Green Onion Sauce

MAKES 1/2 CUP

These flavorings lift a batch of steamed carrots, green snap beans or Chinese long beans, or just about kind of vegetable, for that matter. It makes a fragrant, juicy sauce for steamed, grilled, or pan-fried fish, tofu, chops, and cutlets.

1/4 cup peanut oil or vegetable oil
1/4 cup chopped green onions
1 tablespoon soy sauce
2 teaspoons oyster sauce or a
   pinch of sugar

1/8 teaspoon ground white pepper
1/4 cup vegetable stock or
   chicken broth

Heat oil in a wok or small skillet. Add green onions and stir-fry 2 minutes, until wilted. Add remaining ingredients and mix well. Use immediately.

Per tablespoon: 64 calories, 1 g carbohydrates, trace protein, 7 g fat

Court Bouillon

MAKES 6 CUPS

6 cups water
1 carrot, sliced
1 small onion, sliced

1/2 bay leaf
6 peppercorns
2 tablespoons dry white wine

◼ Combine ingredients in a medium saucepan and heat to boiling over medium heat. Cover and simmer over low heat 15 to 20 minutes. Strain and cool before using.

Per cup: 3 calories, 0 carbohydrates, 0 protein, 0 fat.

Preserved-Lemon Butter

MAKES 12 TABLESPOONS

A variation of the French classic maître d'hôtel butter, this flavoring mix contains Middle Eastern salted lemons. You can add a dollop to sizzling chops, steaks, and fillets, vegetables, and soups.

1/2 cup unsalted butter, softened
1/2 cup chopped parsley

1 to 2 wedges of Preserved Lemons, or to taste, skin only or flesh if desired, finely chopped

◼ Beat the butter until fluffy in a bowl. Stir in parsley and lemon to taste.

Per 11/2 tablespoons serving:103 calories, trace carbohydrates, trace protein, 12 g fat

Hot Citrus Butter

MAKES APPROX. 1 CUP

Perfect for any food that likes a squeeze of lemon juice, and its use of citrus zest packs more flavor than acidity.

1 cup dry white wine
1 teaspoon grated lemon or lime
    zest
1 teaspoon grated orange zest
2 tablespoons fresh lemon or
    lime juice

2 tablespoons fresh orange juice
1/2 cup heavy cream
1/2 cup cold butter, diced
salt and pepper to taste

Combine wine, zest, and juices in small saucepan and boil until reduced to 6 tablespoons. Add cream and simmer until reduced to 1/2 cup, about 5 minutes. Remove pan from heat and whisk in butter, one piece at a time, until melted and sauce is thickened (do not boil). Season with salt and pepper, set aside, and keep warm, not hot, or sauce may separate.

Per 1/4 cup serving: 288 calories, 3 g carbohydrates, 1 g protein, 27 g fat

Cucumber-Dill Butter

Use as a topping for hot fish or chops, mix into bowls of steaming vegetables, or toss with strands of spaghetti squash or yellow squash and zucchini noodles. Think outside the bagel: You can spread this butter onto Boston lettuce, top with thin slices of smoked salmon, and wrap it all up for a low-carb weekend brunch.

1/2 cup unsalted butter, softened

1/4 cup minced, peeled, seeded cucumber

2 teaspoons minced fresh dill

1 1/2 teaspoons fresh lemon juice

Beat butter in a medium bowl with a wooden spoon until creamy. Stir in cucumber, dill, and lemon juice until mixed.

Each 2 tablespoon serving: 137 calories, trace carbohydrates, trace protein, 15 g fat

Montpellier Butter

YIELD 1¹/₂ TO 2 CUPS

You'll have to prepare this versatile condiment when you're not in a hurry—it's worth the effort to have on hand in your freezer. Whisk a knob into a sauce, soup, or bowl of hot vegetable puree; you'll need no other seasoning.

6 leaves spinach
1¹/₂ cups watercress leaves
2 tablespoons fresh Italian
    parsley leaves
2 tablespoons chervil leaves
2 tablespoons chopped fresh chives
1 tablespoon fresh tarragon leaves
2 shallots, chopped
2 cornichons, rinsed and chopped
4 anchovy fillets
2 tablespoons capers

1 garlic clove, peeled
¹/₄ teaspoon cayenne pepper
3 hard-cooked egg yolks
2 large raw egg yolks
¹/₂ cup unsalted butter, softened,
    in bits
¹/₂ cup extra-virgin olive oil
1 teaspoon white wine vinegar
salt and freshly ground white
    pepper to taste

■ Blanch greens, herbs, and shallots in boiling water 1 minute. Drain; refresh under cold water. Squeeze dry; place in food processor. Add cornichons, anchovies, capers, garlic, and cayenne pepper; puree. Add egg yolks and butter; puree. If butter is still in bits, with motor running, pour in oil in a thin steady stream through hole in lid; otherwise, place in a bowl; whisk in oil by hand. Beat in vinegar; add salt and pepper. Adjust seasonings.

Each tablespoon: 93 calories, 5 g carbohydrates, 1 g protein, 10 g fat

Mojo Sauce

There's magic in mojo, this Cuban flavoring mix for meats and fish. It's worth keeping watch for bottled sour orange juice as you travel to different grocery stores; it adds more flavor than just acidity to the resulting sauce.

4 large garlic cloves, crushed
   through a press
1 medium onion, thinly sliced
1/2 cup sour orange juice (from
   Seville oranges); or 1/4 cup
   sweet orange juice and 1/4 cup
   lime juice

1/2 teaspoon salt
1/4 cup Spanish olive oil

■ Mix garlic, onion, juice, and salt in nonreactive bowl. Let stand 30 minutes. Heat oil in a deep saucepan over medium-high heat; add garlic mixture (stand back; it will sputter). Simmer 5 minutes. Serve immediately. Sauce can be stored several weeks in refrigerator; reheat gently and serve warm.

Note: Sour orange juice is available in the specialty foods department of large grocery stores.

Each tablespoon: 75 calories, 3 g carbohydrates, trace protein, 7 g fat

Vegetable Pesto

This paste will make you think of traditional pesto in a new way.

**2 pounds spinach or kale, or 1/2
  cabbage (red or green; Savoy
  is nice)**
4 garlic cloves

3/4 cup extra-virgin olive oil
**1/2 cup grated imported sardo,
  Peccorino-Romano, or
  Parmesan cheese**

▦ Rinse spinach or kale well, drain, and remove stems and thick veins. If using cabbage, core and cut leaves into 1-inch wedges.

▦ Heat 3 quarts water to boiling in a large pot, add enough salt to make the water taste like the sea, and cook the greens for 8 minutes or until tender. Drain, reserving 1/2 cup cooking water; rinse under cold water until cool.

▦ Combine the cooked greens, garlic, olive oil, and cheese in a food processor; pulse, adding reserved cooking water as necessary, until rough paste forms. Use immediately or transfer to a jar; cover with 1/4 inch oil and store in refrigerator up to 2 weeks.

Each tablespoon: 94 calories, 2 g carbohydrates, 2 g protein, 9 g fat

Tzatziki (Greek Yogurt-Cucumber Sauce)

MAKES ABOUT 2 1/2 CUPS

You'll cast mint jelly out of your life forever once you taste this traditional Ionian accompaniment to grilled lamb.

Yogurt Cheese, drained only 4 hours, (see page 170)

2 Kirby cucumber

1/4 teaspoon fine sea salt or to taste

2 tablespoons finely chopped fresh mint or dill

1 tablespoon olive oil, preferably Greek

1 teaspoon vinegar

2 large garlic cloves, crushed through a press

freshly ground white pepper to taste

■ Place Yogurt Cheese in a medium bowl; set aside in refrigerator. Peel and quarter cucumbers; remove seeds with a spoon. Finely dice flesh; place in small bowl. Sprinkle with 1/4 teaspoon salt; toss. Let stand 1 hour. Drain; pat dry with paper towels. Add to Yogurt Cheese with remaining ingredients. Mix well. Taste; adjust seasonings if necessary.

Each tablespoon: 38 calories, 4 g carbohydrates, 3 g protein, 2 g fat

Cajun Spice Rub

MAKES ABOUT 1/4 CUP

You can mix up a spice jar full to have on hand for big jobs like a pork loin or brisket. This is enough for about 6 small fish fillets or boneless pork chops.

1 tablespoon sweet Hungarian
    paprika
2 teaspoons salt
1 teaspoon onion powder
1 teaspoon garlic powder
1 teaspoon cayenne pepper
3/4 teaspoon freshly ground
    white pepper

3/4 teaspoon freshly ground
    black pepper
1/2 teaspoon dried thyme leaves
1/2 teaspoon dried oregano leaves
1/2 teaspoon crushed fennel seeds
1/2 teaspoon celery salt

Mix ingredients in small bowl, using back of a spoon to break up any little lumps. Store, tightly covered, in a jar.

Each teaspoon: 5 calories, 1 g carbohydrates, trace protein, trace fat

Quick Preserved Lemons

You can find preserved lemons in Indian and Middle Eastern grocery stores, and there are recipes for the long process required to ripen fresh lemons. This recipe is a quicker, 5- to 7-day process.

6 lemons
1 cup salt

▧ Cut lemons into 8 wedges each. Stir salt in 1 quart water in medium saucepan until dissolved; add lemons. Cover; heat to boiling over medium heat. Simmer until peels are very soft; let stand until cool. Place lemons in clean jar, cover with cooking brine, and let stand, loosely covered, at room temperature for 5 to 7 days. Store after that in covered jar in refrigerator. Remove lemons as needed. Rinse off brine before using. Discard pulp if desired, but both skin and flesh can be used.

Each wedge (1/8 lemon): 3 calories, 1.4 g carbohydrates, trace protein, trace fat

Roasted Garlic

MAKES 1/4 CUP PUREE

4 to 5 ounces garlic bulbs (2 to 3   **1 tablespoon olive oil**
medium heads)

■ Preheat oven to 500° F. Separate garlic cloves and place in shallow baking dish. Bakes 25 minutes, until skins are crisp and browned and garlic is soft. Press puree out of skins with back of a spoon through a sieve. Place in a small jar, pour oil over top, and store in refrigerator.

Each teaspoon: 18 calories, 4 g carbohydrates, 1 g protein, trace fat

Greek Egg and Lemon Sauce
(Avgolemono)

This tasty sauce is used on lamb, chicken, and fish that is cooked just about any way.

3 eggs	salt to taste
3 tablespoons fresh lemon juice	freshly ground white pepper to
3/4 cup boiling broth or water	taste

■ Beat eggs with the lemon juice in a small saucepan. Whisk in broth gradually; cook over low heat, stirring 3 minutes, until slightly thickened. Sauce will curdle if it boils.

Per serving: 59 calories, 1 g carbohydrates, 5 g protein, 4 g fat

Beef, Veal, and Lamb

Roasted Beef Tenderloin with Morel Sauce

MAKES 8 SERVINGS

This deluxe cut is for serving special company. Combined with the earthy flavor and aroma of morels, the dinner plate is a feast of sensory delights.

1 (3-pound) beef tenderloin, tied
2 tablespoons fresh thyme leaves, finely chopped
2 tablespoons fresh rosemary needles, finely chopped

2 tablespoons extra-virgin olive oil
1/2 teaspoon kosher salt
1/2 teaspoon freshly ground pepper
Morel and Green Peppercorn Sauce, (see page 87)

▓ Preheat oven to 475F degrees; place tenderloin in roasting pan. Combine herbs, oil, salt, and pepper in a cup and mix. Rub over tenderloin. Roast 20 minutes for medium-rare or until an instant-read thermometer inserted in center of roast reads 135° F. Place tenderloin on cutting board; cover with foil.

▓ Let roast stand 15 minutes before cutting into thin slices. Serve with Morel Sauce.

Without sauce, per serving: 381 calories, 0 carbohydrates, 25 g protein, 31 g fat

(See overleaf for recipe photo)

Korean Grilled Beef Short Ribs (Bul-Goki) or Flank Steak

MAKES 8 SERVINGS

Grilling over charcoal is really the way to go here to optimize the marvelous flavor of the marinade. For entertaining or to accommodate busy schedules, the meat can be prepared ahead of time and reheated. Thin slices of the cold flank steak, when tossed with lightly dressed mixed greens, make a mouth-watering main-dish salad any time of year.

6 pounds lean beef short ribs, cut into 1¹/2-inch pieces or a 3-pound flank steak

Marinade:
1/2 cup soy sauce
1/4 cup sugar

2 tablespoons dark sesame oil
1 large garlic clove, crushed through a garlic press
4 large green onions, including fresh green tops, finely chopped
1/2-inch piece grated peeled fresh ginger

■ With a sharp knife, cut through meat almost to the bone in a 1/2-inch-wide checkerboard fashion. For a flank steak, score the sides with a checkerboard of 1/4 inch deep diagonal slashes. Place in a large shallow roasting pan or bowl.

■ In a heavy saucepan, combine marinade ingredients. Heat to a boil over medium-high heat, stirring to dissolve sugar. Remove from heat and cool.

■ Pour marinade over ribs or flank steak and turn to coat. Let stand, turning frequently, 1 to 4 hours.

■ Preheat broiler or prepare outdoor grill for barbecue. Drain meat and broil or grill until desired doneness, turning frequently.

Per serving: 408 calories, 4 g carbohydrates, 40 g protein, 25 g fat

Austrian Stew

This dish is my mother's mother's culinary legacy. It is from the Croatian island of Krk, once part of the Austro-Hungarian Empire—hence the name. The recipe is made with two kinds of meat—always beef, and either chicken or pork, preferably on the bone. Mom always includes chicken drumsticks for her grandchildren.

1/2 cup vegetable oil

2 1/2 pounds sirloin tip, cut into 2-inch chunks

2 medium onions, thinly sliced

2 tablespoons tomato paste

1/2 cup zinfandel or Chianti

1 cup canned Italian tomatoes and juice

2 1/2 pounds chicken parts or country-style pork spareribs or chops

2 cups hot water

1/2 cup plain tomato sauce

1 to 2 garlic cloves, minced

1 tablespoon chopped fresh Italian parsley

1 teaspoon each ground allspice, salt, and dried thyme leaves

1/2 teaspoon each celery salt, ground cloves, freshly ground pepper, and freshly grated nutmeg

freshly grated Parmesan cheese for serving

▓ Heat oil in 6-quart dutch oven over medium-low heat. Add beef and onions; cover; simmer 3 hours, until all juices evaporate.

▓ Stir tomato paste into beef mixture; sauté until sizzling. Stir in wine. Add tomatoes (hold back the juice); crush with back of wooden spoon. Add juice from tomatoes and remaining ingredients except cheese. Mix well. Cover; heat to boiling over medium-high heat. Reduce heat to simmer; cook 20 minutes, until chicken or pork is cooked through. Serve topped with freshly grated Parmesan cheese if desired.

Per serving: 424 calories, 7 g carbohydrates, 50 g protein, 20 g fat

Ropa Vieja

MAKES 6 SERVINGS

The name of this classic Spanish dish translates as "old clothes" because the meat is shredded into raggedy looking pieces. I decided to try it using salsa instead of dealing with all the individual fresh vegetable components (tomatoes, bell pepper, onions, chiles), and I never looked back. This is traditionally served over rice, but I like it over a mound of juicy shredded lettuce.

1 (1½-pound) flank steak or
   skirt steak, cut crosswise into
   2-inch strips
2 garlic cloves, crushed through
   a press

2 cups sugar-free medium-hot
   salsa
2 medium carrots, peeled, halved
   lengthwise, then crosswise
   into 1-inch chunks

■ Mix steak, garlic, and salsa in large dutch oven; heat to boiling over medium-high heat. Cover; simmer over low heat 2 hours, until tender. Heat to boiling; add carrots. Cover; simmer 20 minutes, until carrots are tender.

■ Remove pan from heat; cool 30 minutes. Pull meat into shreds in pan with 2 forks. Stir into pan juices.

Per serving: 209 calories, 7 g carbohydrates, 19 g protein, 11 g fat

Veal with Parma Ham and Sage

MAKES 4 SERVINGS.

These are classic Saltimboca ingredients that are served in rolls—which put a new twist on this Roman favorite.

8 small veal scallops, about 2
  ounces each
4 large or 8 small paper-thin
  slices prosciutto
8 fresh sage leaves

3 tablespoons unsalted butter,
  divided
2 tablespoons extra-virgin olive oil
1/4 cup dry white wine or Marsala
salt and pepper to taste

■ Have your butcher pound out scallops to even thickness. To do it yourself, place scallops 2 inches apart between 2 sheets plastic wrap. Gently pound with meat mallet or rolling pin, to no less than 1/4 inch thickness, being careful not to turn meat fibers into paste.

■ Cover each scallop with a piece of prosciutto; roll up scallop and prosciutto, wrap a sage leaf around the roll and secure with a wooden pick.

■ Melt 2 tablespoons butter in the oil in a large nonstick skillet over high heat until foaming; add scallops; sauté 2 minutes on each side, until cooked through and golden. Place on heated platter. Cover loosely with foil to keep warm.

■ Add wine to skillet and heat to boiling, scraping up browned bits with wooden spoon. Stir in remaining butter, whisking over low heat until melted but not oily. (Do not boil or sauce will separate.) Season to taste. Pour over veal rolls.

Per serving: 231 calories, trace carbohydrates, 22 g protein, 14 g fat

Barbecued Veal Shoulder

MAKES 10 SERVINGS

This roast starts on the grill, where it gets that incomparable flavor of the coals. It finishes up in the oven, in a moist bath of barbecue sauce.

1 (5-pound) boneless veal
   shoulder, untied
3 large garlic cloves, crushed
   through a press
2 bunches green onions, trimmed,
   with some green, chopped
1 large yellow onion, peeled and
   chopped
8 sprigs parsley, chopped
1/2 cup peanut oil

1/2 cup crushed tomatoes
1/2 cup red wine vinegar or
   sherry vinegar
1/4 cup Worcestershire sauce
4 tablespoons honey
1 teaspoon salt
1/2 teaspoon freshly ground
   black pepper
1/4 teaspoon Tabasco sauce

▓ Place meat in a deep baking dish. Heat oil in large skillet over medium heat; sauté vegetables and parsley 5 minutes. Stir in remaining ingredients; simmer 20 minutes. Cool; spread over veal. Cover; refrigerate 5 to 24 hours, turning once or twice.

▓ Prepare outdoor grill for barbecue or preheat broiler. Drain meat; heat marinade in saucepan. Cook meat 4 inches from heat source for 15 minutes, turning every 5 minutes. Heat oven to 375F degrees. Place meat and marinade in cleaned baking dish. Cover; bake 1 to 1 1/2 hours, until tender. Let stand, covered, 10 to 15 minutes before slicing.

Per serving: 308 calories, 8 g carbohydrates, 30 g protein, 17 g fat

Greek-Style Roast Leg of Lamb with Artichokes

MAKES 10 SERVINGS

Time a smaller leg with a general 20 minutes per pound rule; watch and test with an instant-read thermometer to catch it while it's on the rare side.

6- to 7-pound leg of lamb
1 teaspoon kosher salt
1/4 teaspoon freshly ground pepper
3 to 4 garlic cloves, cut into slivers
1/3 cup butter, melted, or Greek olive oil
1/4 cup fresh lemon juice
2 tablespoons dried oregano leaves, crushed

1 cup hot water
1 (10-ounce) package frozen artichoke hearts, thawed
Greek Egg and Lemon Sauce (Avgolemono), (see page 102) or Tzatziki Sauce, (see page 97)

■ Preheat oven to 350° F. Place lamb in roasting pan; sprinkle with salt and pepper. Slit lamb with tip of paring knife and insert garlic slivers, dragging in a little salt and pepper with them. Repeat all over the lamb with the remaining garlic. Rub butter or oil over meat; sprinkle with lemon juice and oregano. Add hot water to pan. Bake 1 1/2 hours, basting every 30 minutes with pan juices. Arrange artichokes around lamb; bake 30 minutes, until internal temperature of lamb registers 130° F for medium rare.

■ When lamb is done, remove to heated platter along with artichokes. Let stand, loosely tented with sheet of foil, for 15 minutes; remove to cutting board for carving. Serve with Greek Egg and Lemon Sauce (Avgolemono) or Tzatziki Sauce.

Without sauce, per serving: 407 calories, 5 g carbohydrates, 48 g protein, 21 g fat

Spanish Lamb Stew with Saffron Cauliflower Couscous

MAKES 4 TO 6 SERVINGS

There are so many flavors going on here, you'd think they would hide the presence of the lamb. But by the time the stew has simmered, every seasoning has mellowed to perfection.

5 garlic cloves, crushed through a press

1 1/2 cups dry red Spanish wine, divided

6 tablespoons extra-virgin Spanish olive oil, divided

1 tablespoon smoked "bittersweet" or sweet Spanish paprika

2 teaspoons chopped fresh thyme leaves

1 teaspoon fine sea salt or more to taste

1/2 teaspoon freshly ground black pepper or more to taste

2 pounds lamb leg or shoulder, cut into 1 1/2-inch cubes

2 onions, finely chopped

1 cup chopped pitted large green Spanish olives

1 tablespoon grated orange zest

Saffron Cauliflower Couscous, (see page 163)

■ Mix garlic, 1/2 cup wine, 4 tablespoons oil, paprika, thyme, 1 teaspoon salt, and 1/2 teaspoon pepper in large bowl. Add lamb; rub marinade on all sides. Cover; refrigerate overnight, stirring every 8 hours. Drain lamb, and reserve marinade.

■ Heat 2 tablespoons oil in large dutch oven over medium heat; brown lamb with onions, in 2 batches, about 2 minutes per batch. Heat lamb, onions, marinade, and remaining wine to a simmer over medium heat; cover. Cook 2 hours, until tender, stirring often. Add olives; simmer 10 minutes, covered, if sauce is thick, and uncovered if it is thin. Serve with Saffron Cauliflower Couscous.

Each of 6 servings, without couscous: 467 calories, 6 g carbohydrates, 24 g protein, 34 g fat

Grilled Butterflied Lamb with Fragrant Spices

MAKES 10 SERVINGS

The aroma alone of the toasted spices as they cook on the meat will dazzle your guests at a backyard barbecue.

1 tablespoon cumin seeds	1/2 teaspoon cayenne pepper
1 tablespoon coriander seeds	2 tablespoons vegetable oil
1 tablespoon black peppercorns	11/2 tablespoons soy sauce
11/2 teaspoons ground turmeric	1 (3 to 41/2-pound) leg of lamb,
1/2 teaspoon ground cinnamon	butterflied

▓ Sauté cumin seeds and coriander seeds in small skillet over medium heat 2 minutes, until fragrant. Add peppercorns, turmeric, cinnamon, and cayenne and sauté 30 seconds. Pour spice mixture into a dish; cool. Pour into heavy plastic food storage bag; seal and pound with rolling pin to crush whole spices. Pour back into bowl; stir in oil and soy sauce.

▓ Place lamb in large glass baking dish; score on both sides with diagonal slashes and rub with spice mixture. Place lamb fat side down in dish, cover with plastic wrap, and refrigerate overnight or for up to 2 days.

▓ Prepare outdoor grill for barbecue or preheat broiler. If desired, weave long metal skewers through lamb to keep it from curling. Place lamb on grill 4 inches from heat source; cover grill. Cook, turning every 5 to 10 minutes, until instant-read thermometer inserted in thickest part of meat registers 125° F to 130° F for medium rare. Remove lamb to heated platter; tent with foil. Let stand 10 to 15 minutes; slice across the grain.

Per serving: 452 calories, trace carbohydrates, 37 g protein, 33 g fat

Broiled Lamb Chops with Preserved-Lemon Butter and Dill

MAKES 4 SERVINGS

There's no point messing with the good thing of perfectly cooked, thick, rib lamb chops. A little bit of tangy butter melting and dripping into the dill infusion is here for dipping.

1 large garlic clove, crushed
   through a press
1 tablespoon olive oil
1/2 teaspoon kosher salt
1/2 teaspoon freshly ground pepper
8 (1- to 1 1/4–inch thick) rib lamb
   chops (3 pounds total)

2 tablespoons Preserved-Lemon
   Butter, or to taste
   (see page 91)
1 tablespoon Dill Oil, (see page
   74) or 1 tablespoon chopped
   fresh dill

■   Preheat broiler. Mix garlic, oil, salt, and pepper; rub over chops. Place chops on rack in broiler pan. Broil 3 inches from heat source 3 to 4 minutes each side for medium-rare. Serve on warm plates topped with big pats of Preserved-Lemon Butter; drizzle with Dill Oil.

Per serving: 545 calories, 0 carbohydrates, 31 g protein, 46 g fat

Orange Lamb and Broccoli Rabe Stir-Fry

MAKES 4 SERVINGS

The spicy, sweet marinade forms a caramelized glaze over slivers of tender lamb. Mung bean cellophane noodles are a neutral backdrop for the mix of bold flavors.

1 pound boneless lamb from the leg, partially frozen and sliced across the grain into 2-inch x 1/8-inch pieces
4 tablespoons peanut oil or corn oil, divided
1 bunch broccoli rabe, with leaves, cut into 1-inch pieces
1/2 cup beef broth
1/2 teaspoon cornstarch

Marinade:
2 tablespoons sweet Chinese chili sauce (or 2 tablespoons rice wine mixed with 1/2 teaspoon chili oil, curry powder, or cayenne pepper)
2 tablespoons soy sauce
2 teaspoons cornstarch
2 teaspoons grated orange zest
1 teaspoon dark sesame oil

▇ Mix marinade in a zip-top plastic bag. Add lamb, close bag, and squeeze to mix. Refrigerate 1 hour to 2 days.

▇ Heat 2 tablespoons oil in wok over high heat until almost smoking. Add broccoli rabe and 2 tablespoons water; stir-fry 4 minutes, until tender. Remove to a bowl.

▇ Heat remaining oil in wok. Add lamb and marinade; stir-fry 3 minutes or until cooked to desired doneness, pressing meat against wok while frying. Mix broth and cornstarch, add, and stir-fry until boiling. Add broccoli; stir until coated with sauce and heated through.

Without noodles, per serving: 379 calories, 6 g carbohydrates, 18 g protein, 31 g fat

Low-Carb Slow-Cooker Venison Stew

MAKES 4 TO 6 SERVING

You can pay a pretty price for farm-raised venison, and we all have come to realize that farm-raised things may not be better than the wild version. If you've never had wild venison, you might want to start out with this very homey choice of life-long hunters.

3 pounds venison, leg or shoulder roast

1 can (about 10 ounces) condensed golden mushroom soup

1 soup can water

1 large onion, sliced

1 large green bell pepper, seeded and sliced

1 tablespoon Worcestershire sauce or to taste

1/4 teaspoon crushed red pepper flakes to taste

1 teaspoon salt or to taste

1/2 teaspoon freshly ground black pepper or to taste

▓ Cut meat into 2-inch pieces; place in slow cooker or crock pot. Add soup; fill can with water, scrape out any soup, and add to cooker. Add onion, bell pepper, Worcestershire sauce, 1 teaspoon salt, and 1/2 teaspoon black pepper. Stir, cover, and cook 8 hours or until tender.

Each of 6 servings: 337 calories, 7 g carbohydrates, 53 g protein, 9 g fat

Pork

Cuban Mojo Pork
(Masitas de Puerco Fritas)

MAKES 4 SERVINGS

Mojo traces back to the African term for medicine man, spell, hex, charm, and magical power. So watch out when you eat this juicy, flavorful Cuban pork with its crisp, chewy crust: you are bound to fall into a trance!

2 pounds pork shoulder or leg
4 garlic cloves, crushed through
   a press
1 teaspoon salt
1/4 teaspoon freshly ground pepper
1/2 cup sour orange juice
   (from Seville oranges)

olive oil for frying
sliced onions for serving
Mojo Sauce, for serving,
   (see page 95), or lime wedges

◾ Cut pork into 1- or 2-inch cubes; place in nonreactive bowl. Rub with garlic, salt, and pepper. Add juice; toss to coat. Cover; refrigerate 3 to 24 hours, turning meat occasionally.

◾ Preheat oven to 200° F. Drain meat. Heat 2 inches oil in heavy dutch oven to almost smoking. Cook pork in batches, raising heat after pork is added to the oil to keep the temperature from dropping. Turn pork until all sides are crisp. (Reduce heat as necessary to keep pork from burning and increase it as necessary when adding second batch.) Remove to paper-towel lined baking pan; keep warm in oven while frying remaining pork. Serve immediately, with onions and Mojo Sauce.

Note: Sour orange juice is available in the specialty foods department of large grocery stores; substitute half sweet orange juice and half lime juice for the amount called for.

Per serving: 280 calories, 0 carbohydrates, 42 g protein, 11 g fat

(See overleaf for recipe photo)

Black and White Pork Chops

These chops are a true flash in the pan, as the coating and their thinness insist on quick cooking. They would make nice appetizers for a hands-on crowd: barely cook them through and keep them warm in a roasting pan, covered with foil in a low oven for up to an hour before serving.

4 (1/4- to 1/2-inch thick) rib pork
   chops, bones frenched
1 egg white
1 tablespoon cornstarch
1/2 teaspoon salt
2 tablespoons mirin or sweet sherry

1/2 cup mixed black and white
   sesame seeds
peanut oil for shallow frying
Fresh Ginger Sauce,
   (see page 86)
fresh cilantro leaves for garnish

■ Mix egg white, cornstarch, mirin, and salt in small bowl until egg white is completely evenly blended. Place pork chops on plate and brush meat on all sides with mixture (don't coat the bones). Let stand 30 minutes.

■ Mix sesame seeds on flat plate. Brush chops again but lightly with egg-white mixture; press chops into the seeds. Let stand 10 minutes.

■ Heat 1/8-inch layer of oil in large heavy nonstick skillet over medium heat; cook chops partially covered 2 to 3 minutes on each side, until crust is browned and chops are barely cooked through. Place Ginger Sauce in individual ramekins for dipping; float a few cilantro leaves in each.

Per serving without sauce: 329 calories, 7 g carbohydrates, 28 g protein, 20 g fat

Chinese-Spiced Brined Roasted Pork Loin

MAKES 6 SERVINGS

The beauty of a pork loin is its leanness, but it can dry out easily, even with TLC. Brining has come to the rescue, and once you've tried it, you'll brine chops, too. Play with the brine; you can make up your own secret house blends of spice and herb combinations.

1 star anise, crushed

2 tablespoons kosher salt

1 teaspoon Szechuan peppercorns

1 teaspoon freshly ground pepper

1 teaspoon ground ginger

1/4 teaspoon cayenne pepper

1/4 teaspoon garlic salt

1/4 teaspoon celery salt

1/4 teaspoon onion salt

1 (3-pound) boneless pork loin with some fat left on top

Heat spices and salt in small skillet over medium heat 5 minutes, until fragrant. Pour into glass measure; add 1 cup boiling water. Stir; let stand until cool. To marinate: Place loin in glass loaf pan large enough to hold the loin without overflowing or a nonreactive baking dish; add brine. Or inject inject brine at intervals into pork loin using cooking syringe; refrigerate 1 to 24 hours.

Remove loin from brine; dry with paper towels and place fat side up in roasting pan. Let pork stand at room temperature 30 minutes. Preheat oven to 350° F.

Roast pork 1 1/4 hours, until internal temperature on instant-read thermometer reads 145° F. Cover loosely with foil; let rest 15 minutes and slice. (The center will be pink because of brining.)

Per serving: 347 calories, 0 carbohydrates, 36 g protein, 22 g fat

Slow-Braised Pork Shoulder with Shiraz and Allspice

MAKES 6 SERVINGS

A friend introduced me to Shiraz on my first visit to Cape Town, and my cooking hasn't been the same since. The rich texture and exotic flavor of the grape matched the game and fruit combinations of the local cuisine, and inspired similar combinations in the northern hemisphere, too. In this dish, keep the fat on the pork if you are inclined; the juicy bits will melt in your mouth.

2 teaspoons kosher salt	**3¹/2-pound pork shoulder, bone in**
1 teaspoon dried thyme leaves	**¹/4 cup extra-virgin olive oil**
1 teaspoon ground allspice	**1 medium onion, thinly sliced**
¹/2 teaspoon freshly ground pepper	**2 tablespoons tomato paste**
3 garlic cloves, crushed through a press	**2 cups Shiraz, Syrah, or Petite Sirah wine**
1 small bay leaf, crushed	

■ Mix seasonings in a cup; rub over pork. Heat oil in dutch oven over medium-high heat; place pork fat-side down in pan. Add onion; cover and simmer 2 hours over medium-low heat, turning pork every 30 minutes, until juices have evaporated.

■ Stir tomato paste into onion mixture; cook, stirring, until sizzling. Stir in wine, scraping up pan drippings. Heat to boiling, cover, and simmer 30 minutes. Remove from heat; let stand 20 minutes. Remove pork to platter; cover with foil. If juices are thin, simmer about 15 minutes. Slice pork and serve with juices.

Per serving: 518 calories, 4.5 g carbohydrates, 41 g protein, 31 g fat

Portuguese Pork and Clams
(Ameijoas con Carne de Porco a Alentejana)

MAKES 4 SERVINGS

I first had this amazing combination of meat and shellfish at an oceanside restaurant in Portugal, just at sunset. I hope your first experience tasting it will be as memorable!

5 teaspoons sweet Hungarian paprika

4 cloves garlic, pureed through a garlic press

1 teaspoon kosher salt

2 tablespoons olive oil

1 1/4 cups dry white wine

2 pounds boneless pork loin, cut into 1-inch cubes

20 small littleneck clams in their shells, purged (see Note)

1 tablespoon cornmeal

2 tablespoons lard, not vegetable shortening (or use more olive oil)

1 cup coarsely chopped onion

2 tablespoons tomato paste

1/4 cup chopped jarred pimentos

■ Mix paprika, garlic, salt, and oil in medium bowl. Add pork; rub in marinade. Add wine. Cover; refrigerate 6 to 24 hours, turning occasionally.

■ Next day: Cover clams and purge of sand (see Note). Drain and rinse. Heat lard in dutch oven over medium-high heat. Drain pork (reserve marinade); brown in batches. Add onion; sauté 5 minutes. Stir in marinade, tomato paste, pimentos, and pork. Cover; simmer over medium heat 20 minutes or until pork is tender.

■ Arrange clams on pork. Heat to boiling, cover, and steam 6 to 8 minutes, until clams open. (Stir once or twice to make space for clams to open.) Remove any unopened clams.

Note: Before using clams, cover with cold water in bowl, sprinkle with 1 tablespoon cornmeal, and let stand 30 minutes to purge of sand. Drain and rinse.

Per serving: 550 calories, 10 g carbohydrates, 51 g protein, 28 g fat

Smoked Ham Steaks or Chops with Cabbage and Juniper Cream Sauce

MAKES 4 SERVINGS

My mother always stretched an amazing number of meals from a ham—fried slices with milk gravy were one of my favorites. This is a jazzed up version of that memorable comfort food.

1 (1½-pound) ham steak, trimmed of fat, or 4 (6- to 8-ounce) smoked pork chops, ¾-inch thick
1 tablespoon olive oil
½ cup dry white wine or more if needed

2 cups ½-inch wide shreds cabbage, preferably Savoy
¼ teaspoon freshly ground pepper
Juniper Cream Sauce, warm (see page 85)
2 tablespoons chopped fresh parsley

▓ Heat oil in large, heavy, nonstick pan over medium-high heat until hot but not smoking. Add steak or chops and cook 1 or 2 minutes on each side, until browned. Remove meat from pan; add wine, and stir to loosen any browned bits. Add cabbage; spread out in a flat pile and sprinkle with pepper. Place meat on top, cover, and simmer 10 minutes, until ham is hot or chops are cooked through, turning meat over after 5 minutes and adding a little wine as necessary to keep the chops moist.

▓ To serve: Pour sauce over meat and cabbage and sprinkle with parsley.

Per serving: 240 calories, 2.5 g carbohydrates, 32 g protein, 10 g fat

Belgian Endive with Ham and Cheese

MAKES 4 SERVINGS

When I went to school in Amsterdam, my Dutch mother made this for special meals. It was the first time I'd ever eaten the pale, juicy leaves and I loved how the bitter flavor went with the sweet ham and cheese.

4 Belgian endive, each about 2½ inches long and heavy for size
8 (2-ounce) slices ham, preferably Westphalian or prosciutto
4 (2-ounce) slices Dutch Gouda or Edam or Swiss Gruyere cheese

1 cup chicken or vegetable broth
2 tablespoons unsalted butter
2 tablespoons fresh lemon juice
1 cup heavy cream
freshly ground pepper

■ Halve endives lengthwise through core to keep leaves intact. Place each half on a slice of ham. Cut cheese slices in half lengthwise; place on endive halves. Wrap ham around endive so that ends are on bottom.

■ Heat broth, butter, and lemon juice to boiling in large deep skillet over medium heat. Place endives in pan, cover, and cook 15 minutes, basting occasionally with pan juices, until paring knife inserts easily in core ends.

■ Meanwhile, simmer cream in another saucepan until reduced to ½ cup.

■ To serve: Place endives on platter; keep warm. Boil cooking liquid over high heat until reduced to 3 tablespoons. Add to cream; pour through strainer over endives.

Per serving: 558 calories, 10 g carbohydrates, 38 g protein, 41 g fat

Wild Mushroom and Country Ham Stroganoff

MAKES 6 SERVINGS

Throughout my cooking life I have noticed that stroganoff has consistently been high on the list of guy food. Why? The sauce goes with any meat and even disguises leftovers. Serve this Stroganoff Gone Wild! over Yellow Squash and Zucchini Noodles, (see page 156), for a low-carb feast.

1/2 cup unsalted butter
2 tablespoons grated onion
11/2 cups roughly slivered, cooked country ham
2 pounds mixed wild or cultivated fresh mushrooms, cleaned and trimmed

freshly grated nutmeg to taste
fine sea salt to taste
freshly ground white pepper to taste
1 (16-ounce) container sour cream
freshly chopped parsley for garnish

■ Melt butter in large nonstick skillet over medium-high heat; add onion and ham and sauté until ham is sizzling. Add mushrooms and seasoning and sauté over medium heat 15 minutes, until mushrooms are golden.

■ Reduce heat to medium, stir in sour cream with wooden spoon until blended, and heat through; do not allow to boil. Taste and adjust seasoning. Sprinkle with parsley.

Per serving: 389 calories, 9 g carbohydrates, 12 g protein, 35 g fat

Poultry

Stir-Fried Spicy Chicken and Celery

MAKES 4 SERVINGS

Have everything chopped, measured, and waiting before you start to cook. It's a dish that's perfect for the cook and family on the go!

6 tablespoons peanut or vegetable oil

6 cloves garlic, cut into match-head-size dice

1 1/2-inch piece peeled fresh ginger, cut into fine dice

1 teaspoon crushed red-pepper flakes (the newer the jar, the hotter the flakes!)

2 (12-ounce) whole chicken breasts, boned and cut into healthy 1-inch chunks

1 1/2 teaspoons salt

2 tablespoons rice wine or dry sherry

2 green onions, sliced into 1/4-inch pieces

1/4 cup water

1/2 teaspoon sugar

4 ribs celery, cut into 1/4-inch dice

1 tablespoon cornstarch mixed with 2 tablespoons water

■ Heat wok over medium-high heat. Add oil and heat until almost smoking. Add garlic and ginger and stir-fry until fragrant, about 30 seconds. Add pepper flakes and stir-fry 30 seconds. Add chicken and salt and stir-fry 1 minute. Add wine and stir-fry 30 seconds. Add green onions and 1/4 cup water and stir-fry 2 1/2 minutes.

■ Cover and reduce heat to medium. Cook 3 minutes.

■ Uncover wok, sprinkle chicken with sugar, and stir-fry 1 minute. Add celery and stir-fry 1 minute. Remix cornstarch mixture and stir into chicken mixture. Stir-fry 1 minute, until glaze is clear and thickened.

Per serving: 352 calories, 6.5 g carbohydrates, 28 g protein, 23 g fat

(See overleaf for recipe photo)

French Roast Chicken

It may look too simple to be fabulous, but the classic way to cook the perfect bird, basting and turning it every 15 minutes, is worth the attention it requires. Cool the chicken at least 15 minutes before carving for the juiciest meat. If you want pieces to snack on or for sandwiches, chill the whole bird thoroughly before jointing and slicing, and bring to room temperature for eating. Picnic fare? Oui, oui!

1 (3- to 4-pound) chicken, rinsed, patted dry
3 tablespoons butter, softened, and a butter stick wrapper if you have one

1 sprig of fresh rosemary or tarragon or several sprigs of fresh thyme
1 teaspoon fine or shards of sea salt
freshly ground pepper
1 cup chicken broth

■ Preheat oven to 400F degrees. Place bird in small roasting pan. Rub chicken well with butter and place remainder inside bird with the rosemary. Sprinkle with salt and pepper. Pour broth around chicken. Tent with butter wrapper, buttered side down; roast 1 hour, turning bird every 15 minutes, basting with pan juices, and repositioning butter paper over top side. Test for doneness by jiggling the drumstick; it should move freely in the socket but not fall out! Remove and let stand at least 15 minutes before attacking.

Per serving: 431 calories, 0 carbohydrates, 66 g protein, 17 g fat

Pecan-Breaded Chicken Cutlets with Mustard Sauce

MAKES 4 SERVINGS

Try this favorite recipe with other kinds of nuts if you prefer. It's a coating that is nice with turkey, veal, and pork cutlets as well as catfish fillets.

4 (6-ounce) chicken cutlets	2 tablespoons safflower oil
salt and freshly ground pepper	1/3 cup sour cream
to taste	1/3 cup chicken broth, white
4 tablespoons butter, divided	wine, or water
3 tablespoons Dijon mustard	chopped fresh parsley for garnish
1 1/2 to 2 cups ground pecans	

▓ Preheat oven to 200° F. Sprinkle chicken with salt and pepper. Melt 2 tablespoons butter in 12-inch nonstick skillet over medium heat. Remove from heat; whisk in 2 tablespoons mustard. Place pecans on plate. Dip cutlets into butter-mustard to coat; coat with pecans, patting them on to help them stick.

▓ Heat 1 tablespoon oil and 1 tablespoon butter in butter mixture in skillet over medium heat until butter melts. Add 2 cutlets; cook 3 minutes, until browned; brown on second side. Remove to shallow baking dish; keep warm in oven while cooking remaining cutlets in remaining 1 tablespoon oil and 1 tablespoon butter.

▓ Spoon off butter and oil and any burned nuts from skillet. If nuts aren't too charred, spoon over cutlets. Add sour cream, chicken broth, and remaining mustard to pan; whisk to loosen any browned bits. Heat until hot but not boiling; season with salt and pepper. Spoon a dollop of sauce onto plates; top with cutlets. Sprinkle with parsley. Pass remaining sauce.

Per serving: 658 calories, 8 g carbohydrates, 32 g protein, 58 g fat

Chickens Fried under Bricks

You can use any weight, such as a heavy skillet, if you don't happen to have bricks on hand.

2 (1 ¼-pound) chickens or any bird of similar weight, backbones removed

3 tablespoons olive oil or vegetable oil

1 teaspoon onion salt or kosher salt

2 tablespoons sour cream

hot or sweet paprika and freshly ground pepper to taste

■ Rinse chickens; pat dry. Flatten chickens with your hand and remove the breastbones with your fingers. Gently pound flat with your hand. Cut off wing tips; fold back wings. Make small slits in skin on both sides of tails; tuck legs into slits.

■ Heat stovetop griddle large enough to cover two burners or two heavy skillets, one over each burner, over medium-high heat. For breast sides: Brush lightly with oil, sprinkle with salt, slather with half the sour cream, and sprinkle with paprika and pepper. When pan is hot, reduce heat to medium; place chickens breast sides down on pan above each burner. Cover each with foil-covered flat bricks or a 2-pound flat-bottomed object (like a cast-iron skillet) large enough to cover an entire chicken.

■ Cook chickens 8 minutes, until they start to brown. (If not browned, increase heat slightly. If browning too quickly, reduce heat slightly.) Remove weights. Prepare back sides as for breast sides with oil, seasonings, and sour cream. Turn chickens over with tongs. Replace weights and fry chickens 10 minutes or until cooked through.

Note: To make more than 2 chickens, hold cooked ones in a 250° F oven while cooking other batches. Chickens can be held in 150° F oven for no more than about an hour without risk of drying out.

Per serving: 543 calories, 1 g carbohydrates, 79 g protein, 23 g fat

Cheese and Chili Chicken

MAKES 6 SERVINGS.

This mix has held on to its appeal since the early days of Tex-Mex cooking. I have done versions that substituted hot Spanish paprika or oregano for the chili powder and roasted red peppers for the green chiles. The cheese is always what I have on hand, from asiago to ricotta salata.

nonstick cooking spray
8 ounces cheddar or Monterey Jack or Monterey Jack with jalapenos
1 large onion
6 boneless, skinless chicken breast halves
1/2 teaspoon salt or to taste

1/2 teaspoon chili powder or to taste
1/4 cup butter
1/4 cup vegetable oil
1 (7-ounce) can green chilies (mild, not jalapenos)
2/3 cup milk

■ Preheat oven to 350° F. Spray a shallow 2-quart baking dish.

■ Shred cheese in processor; place in bowl. Halve or quarter onion; place in feed tube of processor fitted with thin slicing blade. Slice; place on plate.

■ Slice each chicken breast crosswise at an angle into 4 equal pieces; sprinkle with salt and chili powder. Melt butter in oil in large skillet over medium-high heat; sauté chicken 5 minutes, until browned. Place on plate. Sauté onion and green chilies in drippings 5 minutes, until browned. Combine half onion mixture and the milk in processor; puree.

■ Spread half chicken in baking dish; top with half the cheese. Top with onion mixture; sprinkle with remaining cheese. Bake 20 minutes, until cheese melts and browns slightly.

Per serving: 462 calories, 5 g carbohydrates, 38 g protein, 32 g fat

Chinese Fragrant, Crispy Duck

MAKES 4 TO 6 SERVINGS AS PART OF A CHINESE MEAL.

Make the duck ahead of time to the point of frying. Then cut it up and serve.

2 whole star anise, broken into
   small pieces
1/3 cup salt
1/3 cup Szechwan peppercorns
1 (4 1/2-pound) duck, rinsed and
patted very dry
1/2 cup rice wine or dry sherry

3 green onions, trimmed,
   chopped
3-inch piece grated peeled fresh
   ginger
3 tablespoons soy sauce, divided
1 tablespoon flour for dusting
oil for deep frying

■ Heat star anise, salt, and peppercorns in wok over medium heat until fragrant, 5 minutes. Reserve 3 tablespoons mixture; rub remainder over duck. Place in deep bowl that will fit into a wok, steamer, or stockpot; marinate at room temperature (do not refrigerate) 2 hours, turning occasionally. Wipe off salt with paper towels.

■ Pour wine over duck. Mix onions, ginger, and 1 tablespoon soy sauce; rub over duck. Place on steamer rack or basket that allows at least 1 inch of space between water and bowl. (If you do not have a rack that allows this, remove ends of 3 cans (3 inches tall) and place in a cluster with the open sides up in wok. Place bowl on cans.) Heat water to boiling, cover, and steam 2 hours, turning often with strong wooden spoon inserted into body cavity. Top up boiling water as necessary. Remove duck; drain 1 hour.

■ Cut duck in half down breastbone. Brush with remaining soy sauce; sprinkle with flour. Heat 2 inches oil in wok to 365° F. Deep-fry one half at a time skin side down until crisp, about 5 minutes. Drain on paper towels. Cool; cut to yield 12 to 16 pieces. Serve using reserved salt mixture for dipping.

Each of 6 servings: 429 calories, 0 carbohydrates, 24 g protein, 36 g fat

Tea-Smoked Chicken

Here's exotic picnic fare! Try hickory flakes instead of tea and sugar. Smoke 10 minutes. This is usually part of a mix of dishes because it so intensely flavored. A soup, salad, and julienned Yellow Squash and Zucchini Noodles tossed with Fresh Ginger Sauce or Green Onion Sauce would be as much of a banquet as one could handle in ordinary times!

1 (3½-to 4-pound) chicken,
   rinsed, drained and dried
3 tablespoons kosher salt

¼ cup tea leaves
1 tablespoon sugar
2 teaspoons dark sesame oil

■ Two days before serving: Rub chicken with salt; place in deep bowl that will fit into a wok, steamer, or stockpot. Cover; refrigerate 2 days, turning chicken over every 12 hours.

■ Rinse and dry chicken; place in cleaned deep bowl. Place on steamer rack or in steamer basket that allows at least 1 inch of space between water and bowl. (If you do not have a rack that allows this, remove ends of 3 cans (3 inches tall) and place in a cluster with the open sides up in wok. Place bowl on cans.) Heat water to boiling, cover, and steam 45 minutes. Cool chicken; refrigerate until cold.

■ Line wok and lid with foil; sprinkle tea and sugar on bottom. Place oiled rack or two crossed chopsticks in wok; set chicken on top so there is 1 inch of space between tea and chicken. Turn on stove fan and open a window. Cover wok tightly; turn heat to high. When wisps of smoke appear, smoke 5 minutes. Turn off heat; keep wok covered 15 minutes. Remove lid, averting face. Place chicken on plate. Brush with sesame oil. Chill.

■ Cut chicken into 12 pieces, or cut at joints and slice breast. Serve warm, at room temperature, or cold. Chicken will keep several days in the refrigerator.

Per serving: 431 calories, 0 carbohydrates, 66 g protein, 17 g fat

Green-Tea Chicken Wraps

These exotically fragrant and flavored sandwiches are packed with crisp, juicy vegetables.

12 snow peas, strings removed, julienned

2 green onions, white portion and tender green, julienned

1 cup julienned carrot

4 chicken cutlets (about 4 ounces each)

1/2 cup sake or dry white wine

1 tablespoon low-sodium soy sauce

1/2 teaspoon fine sea salt

2 teaspoons gyokuro (finest quality) green tea leaves

12 leaves Boston or Butter lettuce rinsed and dried

1 cup julienned daikon

Green Tea Aioli, as desired (see page 78)

■ Arrange snow peas, onions, and carrot over bottom of large skillet. Place cutlets on top. Mix sake, soy sauce, and salt in a cup and drizzle over culets. Sprinkle with tea leaves.

■ Heat liquid to boiling over medium-high heat. Cover; steam 4 minutes, until chicken is barely cooked through and vegetables are crisp-tender. Remove pan from heat and let stand, covered, 5 minutes.

■ Place cutlets on cutting board; slice crosswise into 1/4 inch wide pieces. Drain vegetables; place on platter. Spread each lettuce leaf with Green Tea Aioli to taste. Spoon vegetables into each leaf, dividing evenly; top each with one-third of a cutlet and some daikon. Place 3 filled leaves on each serving plate. To eat, fold lettuce over filling.

Per serving without aioli: 189 calories, 9 g carbohydrates, 29 g protein, 2 g fat

Pan-Fried Sake Duck Breasts

MAKES 4 SERVINGS.

This could make a first course for 6 or, with more daikon or greens, a main-course salad for 4.

2 large boneless duck breast halves
3 tablespoons soy sauce
1 teaspoon salt
1 teaspoon ground ginger
1 teaspoon plus 1 tablespoon
    powdered wasabi (Japanese
    radish)

¹/₂ cup sake
2 cups julienned daikon or frisée,
    watercress, mizuna, endive or
    a mix
toasted sesame seeds for garnish
picked ginger slices for serving

■ Score flesh side of duck in ¹/₂-inch crisscross pattern ¹/₄ inch deep. Mix soy sauce, salt, ginger, and 1 teaspoon wasabi and rub into flesh. Place sake in deep bowl and set duck flesh side down in sake. Marinate 4 hours in refrigerator; remove 2 hours before cooking.

■ Heat heavy large, skillet over low heat. Place duck skin side down in pan (reserve sake). Cook very slowly to render fat and brown skin, basting meat with hot fat to cook from top. Cook 20 minutes for medium-rare. Remove to cutting board; cover and let rest 15 minutes. Pour fat from pan. Add sake; boil to reduce to ¹/₄ cup.

■ Arrange daikon or greens on large plates; thinly slice duck breasts and place on top. Sprinkle with sesame seeds. Mix remaining 1 tablespoon wasabi with reduced sake; drizzle around plate. Garnish with pickled ginger.

Per serving: 459 calories, 4 g carbohydrates, 45 g protein, 20 g fat

Roasted Duck with Glazed Radishes

MAKES 4 SERVINGS.

Turnips are a classic French companion to roasted duck, but they have nearly twice the carbs as—radishes! No joke, the darlings of the crudité platter can be cooked, and here they're roasted turnip-tender, basted with delicious duck fat!

1 (4½-pound) duck, quartered
2 large red onions, sliced into
   ½-inch thick rings
8 large red radishes, trimmed
2 tablespoons sherry vinegar or
   balsamic vinegar

2 teaspoons minced fresh
   rosemary leaves
2 teaspoons salt
½ teaspoon freshly ground
   pepper

■ Preheat oven to 400° F. Pull off excess fat from duck. Score skin and flesh sides of duck in ½-inch crisscross pattern ¼ inch deep. Rub with vinegar; sprinkle with rosemary, salt, and pepper. Spread onions in shallow roasting pan; add ½ cup water.

■ Heat large skillet over medium-high heat. Place duck pieces skin side down in pan; cook 5 minutes, until crisp. Place duck leg quarters skin side up on onions. Scatter radishes around duck. Roast 20 minutes, basting duck, onions, and radishes with pan juices. Place breast pieces skin side up in with legs and vegetables; roast 10 minutes.

■ Drain off pan juices; discard liquid fat. Baste duck and vegetables with pan juices, reserving extra juices. Roast duck and vegetables 15 to 20 minutes, until breast is to desired doneness, legs and vegetables are tender and glazed. To serve, drizzle pan juices over duck and vegetables.

Per serving: 256 calories, 8 g carbohydrates, 27 g protein, 13 g fat

Fish

Pepper-Crusted Salmon with Hot Citrus Butter

MAKES 4 SERVINGS

4 teaspoons coarse ground black pepper

4 (6- to 8-ounce) salmon fillets with skin on

2 tablespoons olive oil

1/2 teaspoon salt

Hot Citrus Butter, (see page 92)

■ Press pepper mixture onto skin side of fillets. Sprinkle fish with salt. Heat oil in large nonstick skillet over medium-high heat until almost smoking. Place the salmon, skin side down, in the pan. Cook until skin is crisp, about 2 minutes. Turn salmon over; cook until golden, about 2 minutes. Fish will be medium-rare inside; cook longer if desired, adding an extra minute on the skin side and up to 5 minutes on the second, reducing heat to medium after turning fish. Transfer fish to a warm platter. Sprinkle with 1/2 teaspoon salt and serve with Citrus Butter.

Each serving without sauce: 334 calories, 0 g carbohydrates, 36 g protein, 20 g fat

(See overleaf for recipe photo)

Red Snapper with Ginger and Lemongrass

Thick salmon fillets or cod make delicious alternatives to the snapper. For vegetarian guests who do not eat fish, fry "fillets" of pressed tofu; they are delicious and will be much appreciated.

1 (15-ounce can) coconut milk

6 kaffir lime leaves

1/2 cup finely chopped lemongrass or 3 tablespoons fresh lemon juice

1 tablespoon Vietnamese or Thai fish sauce (or salt)

2 tablespoons olive oil

4 red snapper fillets (6 ounces each), with skin on

fine sea salt to taste

freshly ground white pepper

1 teaspoon ginger juice

shredded Thai or other basil leaves for garnish

■ Preheat oven to 400° F. Combine coconut milk, lime leaves, lemongrass, and fish sauce in small saucepan over medium heat; simmer until sauce is thickened, about 10 minutes.

■ Meanwhile, heat oil in a large ovenproof skillet over medium-high heat. Sprinkle snapper with salt and pepper; place skin side down in skillet. Press fillets with metal spatula and hold down for 1 minute so skin stays flat. Cook 3 minutes, until skin is crisp; turn over. Cook 1 minute and place in oven to finish cooking, about 3 minutes.

■ When sauce has thickened, stir in the ginger juice; season to taste with salt and white pepper. Place snapper fillet skin side up on serving plates; pour some sauce around each. Garnish with basil leaves.

Each filet: 443 calories, 3 g carbohydrates, 37 g protein, 32 g fat

Blackened Catfish with Cucumber-Dill Butter

MAKES 4 SERVINGS

This is a classic dish that New Orleans chef Paul Prudhomme made famous. Salmon, sea scallops, pompano, and red snapper can also be used. Adjust the cooking time according to the thickness of the fish.

3/4 cup unsalted butter

4 (1/2 inch thick, 8 to 10-ounce) catfish fillets, preferably with skin on

Cajun Spice Rub, (see page 98)

Cucumber-Dill Butter, (see page 93)

▨ Have stove fan on high and a window open. Melt butter in large skillet. Dip fillets in butter, drain, and place on cutting board. Sprinkle spice rub on both sides of each fillet and rub it into the fish.

▨ Heat stovetop griddle large enough to cover two burners or two heavy skillets over each burner over high heat until smoking. Place 2 fillets skin side down on each portion of griddle over a burner. Spoon about 1 tablespoon melted butter on top on top of each fillet. Cook 2 minutes, until underside is charred. Turn fish over and cook 2 minutes, until charred on second side. Serve on warm plates with a dollop of Cucumber-Dill Butter on top of each fillet.

Each serving without sauce: 510 calories, 0 carbohydrates, 36 g protein, 40 g fat

Fish Panfried in Parsley Oil with Grape Tomatoes

MAKES 4 SERVINGS

Certain fish need a little more embellishment. The red and green colors brighten up the white fillets and they flavor them at the same time.

2 teaspoons cracked black pepper	1/4 cup Parsley Oil, more if
2 tablespoons grated lemon zest	needed (see page 74)
2 pounds flounder or other	1 cup mixed red and yellow grape
flat fish fillets	or pear tomatoes, halved

▓ Preheat oven to 200° F. Mix pepper and lemon zest on waxed paper and pat onto fish fillets. Heat 1/4 cup Parsley Oil in large skillet over medium-high heat until almost smoking. Add 2 fish fillets and cook 1 to 2 minutes, until lightly browned; turn over and cook 1 to 2 minutes. Place on baking sheet and keep in oven while frying remaining fish.

▓ When fish is done and warming in oven, heat oil in pan to high; add 1 to 2 more tablespoons oil if pan is not glazed from fish. Add tomatoes and sauté 1 minute, until heated through. Pour over fish.

Per serving: 338 calories, 2 g carbohydrates, 43 g protein, 17 g fat

Bay Scallop and Fennel-Lemon Hash

MAKES 6 SERVINGS

Two pounds mixed diced fish and shellfish will make a sublime substitute for scallops.

2 medium bulbs fennel	1/2 cup minced fresh parsley
1/3 cup extra-virgin olive oil	2 tablespoons grated lemon zest
1/2 cup heavy cream	1 tablespoon grated orange zest
2 tablespoons unsalted butter	sea salt to taste
2 pounds fresh bay scallops	freshly ground white pepper to
3 medium cloves garlic, minced	taste

▓ Cut off stalks from fennel; cut fern into 2-inch pieces and reserve. Cut bulbs into 1/4-inch dice. Heat oil in large nonstick skillet over medium-high heat; add fennel and sauté 8 to10 minutes, until golden and crisp-tender. Pour into a bowl. Add cream to pan; boil, stirring until cream is reduced to 1/4 cup. Add to fennel.

▓ Wipe out pan, add butter, and melt over medium-high heat; sauté scallops 2 minutes. Add garlic; sauté 1 minute or just until scallops are opaque. Add sautéed fennel, the parsley, lemon zest, and orange zest; season with salt and pepper, sprinkle with reserved fennel fern, and serve.

Per serving: 325 calories, 9 g carbohydrates, 27 g protein, 20 g fat

Crab or Shrimp Newberg Gratin

MAKES 4 SERVINGS

What an indulgence! As you read the list of rich ingredients, you will cry, "Yes! Yes! Yes!" You can easily stretch the dish for an extra guest or two; serve it with low-carb Yellow Squash and Zucchini Noodles or a bed of Cauliflower Couscous.

1 pound lump crabmeat or large shrimp, peeled, deveined, tails removed

1/2 cup unsalted butter plus extra for buttering dishes

2 cups heavy cream

1/4 cup dry sherry, dry white vermouth, or dry white wine

1 tablespoon fresh lemon juice

1/2 teaspoon Creole or Maryland fish seasoning mix, hot paprika, or hot pepper sauce, to taste

2 whole eggs

2 egg yolks

1 cup shredded cheddar, Gruyère or Swiss cheese or a mixture of cheeses

■ Pick through crab and discard any shells. Cut shrimp into 1/2-inch pieces. Butter 4 small soufflé or gratin dishes

■ Preheat broiler. Melt 1/2 cup butter in a large skillet over medium-high heat and add crab or shrimp. Simmer, stirring 2 to 3 minutes, until crab is sizzling or shrimp just start to curl and turn pink.

■ Combine cream, sherry, lemon juice, seasoning, eggs, and egg yolks in a medium bowl. Whisk until blended. Pour into hot crab mixture and heat, stirring, until custard is almost set and mixture is almost to boiling. Spoon into prepared dishes. Sprinkle with cheese, dividing evenly (about 1/4 cup per serving). Place on a large baking sheet. Broil 2 inches from heat source until cheese melts and browns lightly, about 2 minutes.

Per serving: 672 calories, 7 g carbohydrates, 39 g protein, 53 g fat

Broiled Shrimp Scampi

MAKES 4 SERVINGS

Because it is unusual in America to find the crustaceans called scampi, use the largest shrimp you can find. If they are much smaller than the general 5/6 count suggested, make sure you adjust the cooking time accordingly so the shrimp don't get tough. Use color as a general indicator: When the shells turn pink, it's time to pull them from the heat.

10 large scampi or (5/6-count) colossal shrimp, shell on, split lengthwise; deveined; feet removed
5 tablespoons extra-virgin olive oil
salt and freshly ground pepper to taste

2 tablespoons butter
4 cloves garlic, thinly sliced
1/2 cup dry white wine
2 tablespoons lemon juice
pinch dried red-pepper flakes
1/2 cup chopped fresh parsley

Preheat broiler. Place scampi cut sides up in a broiler pan. Drizzle with 4 tablespoons oil; sprinkle with salt and pepper. Broil about 4 inches from heat source until shells are red and flesh is almost cooked through, about 5 minutes.

While scampi cook, heat remaining oil and butter in small skillet over medium-high heat. Add garlic; heat until fragrant, about 30 seconds. Add wine, lemon juice, and pepper flakes and heat to boiling.

When scampi are cooked, remove from heat, sprinkle with parsley, and drizzle with wine mixture. Broil until sizzling and fragrant, about 1 minute. Serve immediately.

Per serving: 270 calories, 2 g carbohydrates, 8 g protein, 24 g fat

Florence's Salt and Pepper Shrimp

MAKES 4 SERVINGS

This recipe is from Florence Lin. I studied with her at the China Institute in America in New York City many years ago, and I still use her books as a major reference. This classic Chinese dish continues to make the rounds at trendy New York restaurants.

1 pound medium (25 count) unpeeled, headless shrimp
3¹/2 teaspoons kosher salt, divided
1 cup cold water
1 green onion, finely chopped
1 teaspoon freshly ground white pepper
pinch of sugar
oil for frying

▨ Trim feet from shrimp. With kitchen shears, cut lengthwise through the curved back of shells. Remove veins. Dissolve 2 teaspoons salt in 1 cup water in a bowl. Add shrimp; soak 1 hour in refrigerator.

▨ Combine green onion, remaining 1¹/2 teaspoons salt, the pepper, and sugar in a cup. Drain shrimp and pat dry on paper towels. Heat 2 inches oil in a wok or deep skillet to 400° F. Fry half the shrimp at a time until pink and shells are crisp. Drain on paper towels.

▨ Drain off all but 1 tablespoon oil but reserve 1 tablespoon oil for second batch of shrimp. Heat on high until hot. (Heat must be high for shells to get crisp.) In 2 batches, stir-fry half the shrimp with half the onion mixture until shells are very crispy. Remove to serving platter. The shrimp are eaten with shells on.

Per serving: 155 calories, 2 g carbohydrates, 23 g protein, 5.5 g fat.

Chinese-Style Steamed Fish

MAKES 2 TO 3 SERVINGS OF WHOLE FISH AND 3 TO 4 SERVINGS OF FILLETS AND STEAKS.

The flavorful seasoning mix works for just about any kind of white fish, from whole small fish such as sea bass, spot, or porgies; delicate flounder fillets; or thick cod steaks. The key is to use the Canadian method of cooking fish, that is, to cook it by any method for 10 minutes per inch. So if you ever need to turn a fish when you bake, grill, or broil it, time it so you do it halfway through the cooking.

1 1/2 pounds whole fish on the bone, fillets, or steaks
1/2 to 1 teaspoon salt

Steaming Sauce
1 green onion, trimmed and cut into 2-inch slivers
1 tablespoon grated peeled fresh ginger

1 tablespoon soy sauce
1 tablespoon dry sherry or rice wine
1 tablespoon peanut oil or olive oil
2 teaspoons fish sauce (nuoc mam or nam pla), oyster sauce, or dark sesame oil (optional)
pinch of sugar

▆ Rinse fish under gently running cold water and pat dry with paper towels. If using whole fish, make 2 to 3 diagonal slashes to the bone on both sides. Sprinkle fish inside and out with 1 teaspoon salt. For fillets and steaks, remove skin; rinse, dry, and sprinkle flesh with 1/2 teaspoon salt. Place fish in a deep bowl that will fit into a wok or steamer. Place bowl in wok or steamer over boiling water.

▆ Combine sauce ingredients and mix well. Pour over fish. Cover and steam until cooked through, allowing 10 minutes per inch thickness of fish, 5 to 15 minutes. Carefully remove lid and serve immediately.

Per serving: 286 calories, 4 g carbohydrates, 43 g protein, 9 g fat.

Pasta

Yellow Squash and Zucchini Noodles

MAKES 4 SERVINGS

You can vary the thickness of the squash slices according to your pleasure: fettuccine, linguine, pappardelle, lasagna, and short lengths, too. Use a ripple-edge pastry wheel to make curly edges.

8 ounces yellow summer squash,   8 ounces zucchini, ends trimmed
   ends trimmed

■ Cut squashes into long, paper-thin slices on a mandolin or by hand using a thick vegetable parer. (Quarter squash lengthwise if using parer; set quarters on work surface and drag parer along the length.) Cut into widths as desired.

■ Cook "noodles" in a saucepan of boiling salted water about 30 seconds; drain in colander. Rinse with cold water to stop cooking if using noodles for casseroles.

Note: To microwave: Place "noodles" in shallow glass baking dish with 1/4 cup water. Cover with plastic wrap; vent. Cook on HIGH 2 to 3 minutes, stirring gently after 1^{1}/2 minutes. Drain in colander. Rinse with cold water if using noodles for casseroles.

Per serving: 19 calories, 4 g carbohydrates, 1 g protein, trace fat

(See overleaf for recipe photo)

Squash-Fettuccine Alfredo

MAKES 4 SERVINGS

You can "Alfredo" just about any pasta or vegetable; the secret is to have all the sauce ingredients at room temperature, waiting for the vegetable or pasta to emerge from its cooking water.

4 tablespoons unsalted butter, at room temperature

Yellow Squash and Zucchini Noodles, cut the thickness of fettuccine, uncooked, (see opposite page)

1 cup heavy cream, at room temperature

1/4 cup freshly grated Parmesan or Romano cheese or more if needed

Place butter in serving bowl; break up into small pieces. Cook noodles as recipe directs, drain, and toss with butter until all butter is melted. Pour in half the cream; toss with wooden salad tongs to coat. Sprinkle with 1/4 cup cheese; toss. Add more cream if needed; toss to mix. Sprinkle with more cheese before serving.

Per serving: 126 calories, 7 g carbohydrates, 7 g protein, 9 g fat

Spaghetti Squash Noodles

Vitamin-rich squash makes a versatile low-carb replacement for wheat pasta. These juicy, crisp-tender strands serve as a great canvas for all kinds of sauces.

1 (3-pound) spaghetti squash

■ Preheat oven to 375° F. Halve squash lengthwise; scoop out seeds. Place squash halves cut sides up in roasting pan; cover tightly with foil. Bake 1 hour or until tender. Scoop out spaghetti with fork. To microwave: Halve squash lengthwise; scoop out seeds. Place squash halves cut sides up in glass baking dish; add 1/4 cup water to dish. Pierce squash on all sides with fork or metal skewer. Cover with plastic wrap; vent. Cook on HIGH 10 minutes, turning dish every 4 minutes, until tender. Let stand 5 minutes. Scoop out spaghetti with fork.

Each cup: 35 calories, 8 g carbohydrates, 7 g protein, 1 g fat

Spaghetti Squash with Vegetable Pesto

Of course you can use your favorite pesto with spaghetti squash; this variation on the basil classic is just a suggestion. Savoy cabbage is one of my favorite vegetables and it shines with a little ham in its presence.

3 cups Spaghetti Squash Noodles, hot, with reserved cooking water, (see opposite page)

1 recipe Vegetable Pesto, made with Savoy cabbage, (see page 96)

2 ounce paper-thin prosciutto or other ham, shredded (optional)

salt and freshly ground pepper to taste

1/4 cup grated Peccorino-Romano cheese for serving

Combine hot squash in large bowl with pesto; toss with salad forks to coat, adding enough squash cooking liquid to make sauce a juicy, coating consistency. Sprinkle with prosciutto; toss to mix. Taste and season with salt and pepper if necessary. Pass grated cheese to sprinkle as desired.

Per serving: 357 calories, 10 g carbohydrates, 9 g protein, 22 g fat

Vegetable Stir-Fry on Squash Lo Mein

MAKES 4 SERVINGS

The dramatic array of vegetables is as tasty and fragrant as it is beautiful. Substitute fresh vegetables according to season. Have everything cut and measured before you fire up the wok.

3 tablespoons vegetable oil

2 large garlic cloves, crushed through a press

1 teaspoon minced peeled fresh ginger

1/8 teaspoon crushed red pepper flakes

1 cup broccoli florets

1 large green onion, trimmed, quartered lengthwise, cut into 1-inch pieces

2 ounces snow peas, strings removed, julienned

1/2 small red bell pepper, julienned

3 tablespoons low-sodium soy sauce

3 cups Spaghetti Squash Noodles, hot, (see page 158)

■ Heat oil in wok or large skillet over medium-high heat; add garlic, ginger, and pepper flakes and stir-fry 30 seconds, until fragrant. Add broccoli, onion, snow peas, and pepper strips; stir-fry 3 minutes, until crisp-tender. Add soy sauce; stir-fry 2 minutes, until heated through.

■ Place hot squash on serving platter; top with stir-fry.

Per serving: 141 calories, 10 g carbohydrates, 2 g protein, 11 g fat

Spaghetti Pie

MAKES 6 SERVINGS

This dish suggests the idea of a macaroni and cheese stand-in but it is a vegetable casserole unto itself. Feel free to add more of your favorite cheeses to the mix.

butter for greasing dish
2 tablespoons olive oil
1 medium red onion, chopped
1 large garlic clove, crushed
    through a press
1 1/2 cups shredded zucchini
1 (4-ounce) jar roasted red
    peppers, drained and chopped
3 cups cooked spaghetti squash
1/2 teaspoon salt

1/4 teaspoon freshly ground
    black pepper
3 eggs
1 cup half-and-half
1 cup shredded cheese or mixed
    cheeses of your choice
    (cheddar, mozzarella, Jack,
    gruyere, etc.)
1/4 cup grated Romano cheese

■ Preheat oven to 350° F. Butter a shallow 2-quart casserole.

■ Heat oil in large skillet over medium-high heat, add onion, and sauté 7 minutes, until soft. Add garlic; sauté 30 seconds, until fragrant. Add zucchini; sauté 2 minutes, until it starts to wilt. Stir in peppers, squash, salt, and pepper; mix well. Remove pan from heat; cool.

■ Whisk eggs with half-and-half in large bowl until foamy; stir in shredded cheese. Add vegetables; mix well. Pour into prepared dish; sprinkle with Romano. Bake 30 minutes, until set in center.

Per serving: 239 calories, 10 g carbohydrates, 11 g protein, 18 g fat

Cauliflower Couscous

MAKES 4 SERVINGS

What a chameleon cauliflower can be! Here it has just enough visual and al dente qualitites to stand in for the pasta of Northern Africa.

1/4 cup extra-virgin olive oil
1/2 cup chopped shallots
2 cups grated cauliflower

fine sea salt to taste
hot water as necessary

▓ Heat oil in medium nonstick skillet over medium-high heat. Add shallots; sauté 4 minutes, until tender. Add cauliflower, sprinkle with salt and enough water to moisten mixture, and sauté 1 minute, until hot, adding more water as necessary.

Saffron Cauliflower Couscous

MAKES 4 SERVINGS

▓ Crush 1/2 teaspoon saffron threads in glass; measure with back of spoon; add 11/2 cups boiling water and steep 10 minutes. Use to moisten couscous while cooking. Garnish with 1/2 cup toasted chopped blanched almonds.

Per serving: 246 calories, 7 g carbohydrates, 5 g protein, 23 g fat

Tofu Gnocchi with Four Cheeses

MAKES 4 SERVINGS

Repeated visits to Trieste, Italy, has me dreaming of the potato gnocchi with four cheeses I had at a restaurant near my hotel. This is a variation on the recipe the owner gave me.

1 (1-pound) package firm tofu	1/3 cup shredded Dutch Edam
butter for greasing dishes	1/3 cup mascarpone
2 cups heavy cream	1/3 cup grated Parmesan cheese
1/3 cup crumbled Gorgonzola	plus extra for sprinkling

■ Remove tofu from package; place in shallow baking dish. Weight down with loaf pans with a couple soup cans in them; let stand 20 minutes. Drain off liquid; dry out dish. Wrap tofu block with double-thickness paper towels; place in dish and weight down again for 10 minutes.

■ Preheat broiler. Butter 4 (2-cup) ramekins or gratin dishes.

■ Dry tofu again with paper towels. Cut into 1-inch x 3/4-inch pieces. Place on a bowl in a steamer set over boiling water; steam 5 minutes.

■ Meanwhile, heat cream and cheeses in nonstick skillet over medium heat. Whisk 5 minutes, until cheeses melt into the cream and sauce is smooth. Add tofu to sauce and gently toss to coat. Spoon into ramekins or dishes and place under broiler for 3 minutes, or until browned and bubbly. Sprinkle with extra Parmesan cheese for serving.

Per serving: 388 calories, 10 g carbohydrates, 21 g protein, 31 g fat

Nude Ravioli! (Ravioli Nudi!)

MAKES 6 SERVINGS

These pastaless ravioli are also called malfatti, from the Italian for "badly made," as in badly made ravioli. Moniker aside, it's hard not eat the whole batch by yourself. (And you don't have to close your eyes while you eat them!)

15 to 16 ounces best-quality
  fresh whole-milk ricotta
3 (10-ounce) packages frozen
  spinach, thawed
5 egg yolks
1 whole egg
1/4 cup almond flour plus
  more for shaping

1/4 teaspoon salt or to taste plus
  extra for cooking
1/2 teaspoon freshly grated nutmeg
1/4 teaspoon freshly ground pepper
1/2 cup butter
24 sage leaves
1/4 cup sliced almonds
freshly grated Parmesan cheese

▓ Place cheese in cheesecloth-lined sieve placed over a bowl. Weight cheese by placing a plate with a 1-pound can of something on top. Let drain overnight.

▓ Spread spinach on clean tea towels; roll up. Twist to dry. Place spinach in large bowl; add ricotta. Mix well. Stir in egg yolks, egg, 1/4 cup almond flour, 1/4 teaspoon salt, the nutmeg, and pepper. Sprinkle cutting board with almond flour. Drop about 2 dozen rounded spoonfuls of mixture into flour; roll to coat.

▓ Melt butter in small skillet over medium heat; add sage and almonds. Cook 30 seconds.

▓ Heat 8 cups salted water to boiling in a large pot. Cook ravioli 8 minutes, until floating. Remove to warm platter. Reheat sage butter; pour over ravioli. Sprinkle with cheese.

Per serving: 381 calories, 10 g carbohydrates, 17 g protein, 31 g fat

Eggs and Cheese

Curry Cheese–Stuffed Deviled Eggs with Candied Ginger

SERVES 4 TO 6

The recipes that endure are the ones that touch someone's heart as well as their stomachs! This is a modestly glamorized version of what I consider to be the best basic devilled egg.

6 large eggs (If you want to be uppity, use 12 quail eggs; cook only 5 minutes)

1 (8-ounce) package cream cheese, softened

1/2 teaspoon curry powder

1/4 teaspoon dry mustard

1/4 cup chopped almonds, toasted

2 tablespoons finely chopped candied ginger, cut into small pieces

■ Place eggs in a pan large enough to hold them in a single layer; cover with cold water. Heat to boiling over medium-high heat, cover, turn off the heat and let eggs sit 15 minutes. Drain and run under cold water until eggs are completely cool.

■ Peel eggs and cut in half lengthwise. Place yolks in bowl. Add cream cheese, curry powder and mustard; beat until smooth. Cover; refrigerate several hours so flavors can blend. Let spread stand at room temperature about 30 minutes before serving to soften.

■ To serve: Place curry mixture in pastry bag fitted with large star tip; pipe into centers of egg whites. Mix almonds and ginger in a cup; sprinkle over eggs.

Each of 6 servings: 244 calories; 3.5 g carbohydrates, 20g protein, 21 g fat

(See overleaf for recipe photo)

Pimiento Cheese Spread

MAKES ABOUT 2 CUPS

This Southern sandwich filling appears in high and low places, from lunchboxes to social teas. With a peanut-butter texture, it is very lickable from the groove of a beautiful green juicy celery stick. It makes a low-carb sandwich inside a lettuce-leaf wrap.

8 ounces mild yellow cheddar cheese
8 ounces white sharp cheddar cheese
1 (7-ounce) jar chopped pimentos
1 cup roughly chopped green onions
3/4 cup mayonnaise or more to taste

2 tablespoons Worcestershire sauce
1 tablespoon fresh lemon juice
cayenne pepper to taste
raw vegetables or lettuce leaves for serving

■ Shred cheese through the largest holes in grater into large bowl. Add remaining ingredients; whisk until smooth. Serve at room temperature.

Per tablespoon: 82 calories; 2 g carbohydrates, 4 g protein, 7 g fat

Yogurt Cheese

MAKES 1 1/2 CUPS (24 TABLESPOONS)

Wherever there is yogurt, there is yogurt cheese. It is surprising how much liquid comes out with draining! The tangy fresh "cheese" is a versatile medium for seasonings.

1 quart plain yogurt
1/2 teaspoon salt

■ Line large sieve with double-thickness of cheesecloth; set sieve over bowl. Add yogurt; sprinkle with salt and mix in; cover with plastic wrap; refrigerate overnight.

Per tablespoon: 44 calories; 3 g carbohydrates, 2 g protein, 3 g fat

Akuri (Parsi-Style Scrambled Eggs)

MAKES 2 TO 3 SERVINGS

A lifelong carnivore, I spontaneously went vegetarian when I traveled through Nepal and India. Eggs popped up in some of the most interesting and delicious dishes I've ever eaten. This is a representative sample.

6 large eggs
1/4 teaspoon salt
1/8 teaspoon freshly ground pepper
pinch of ground turmeric
3 tablespoons clarified butter
1 large onion, finely chopped
1 garlic clove, crushed through
    a press

1 jalapeno pepper, finely chopped
1 teaspoon grated peeled fresh
    ginger
1 small tomato, peeled, seeded,
    and finely chopped
3 tablespoons finely chopped
    fresh cilantro

Lightly beat eggs in a bowl with salt, pepper, and turmeric. Heat butter in a nonstick skillet over medium heat until hot; sauté onion, garlic, jalapeno, and ginger 5 minutes, until softened and fragrant. Add tomato; sauté 1 minute. Stir in eggs; cook, stirring frequently until egg is just set. Sprinkle with cilantro and serve.

Each of 3 servings: 276 calories; 7 g carbohydrates, 14 g protein, 22 g fat

Grilled Leek and Gruyère Frittata

MAKES 4 TO 6 SERVINGS

Comfort food alert! The bright flavor of leeks and nutty tones of my favorite cheese are together in one dish. It's a perfect dish for a gathering of family and friends.

4 leeks or fat green onions
olive oil for brushing
10 eggs
1/4 cup heavy cream
1/2 teaspoon salt

1/4 teaspoon freshly ground
   pepper or to taste
1 cup shredded Gruyère cheese
3 tablespoons butter

▨ Preheat broiler. Trim ends and tough green portions from leeks. Cut in half lengthwise, rinse very well under running water to remove grit. Place in shallow roasting pan, brush with oil, and broil 8 minutes 6 inches from heat, until charred and tender, brushing with oil and turning every 3 minutes. Remove to cutting board; cut into 1 1/2-inch lengths.

▨ Preheat oven to 350° F. Whisk eggs, cream, salt, and pepper in large bowl until blended. Stir in leeks and Gruyère.

▨ Heat 2 tablespoons butter over medium-low heat in 10-inch heavy skillet with heat-resistant handle. Add egg mixture and cook 3 minutes, lifting up from bottom with a spatula as eggs set. Bake 10 minutes, or just top is set. With spatula, loosen from bottom and around edge, and slide onto serving platter. Cut into wedges.

Each of 6 servings: 319 calories; 10 g carbohydrates, 17 g protein, 24 g fat

Smoked Haddock Omelet with Sorrel Cream Sauce

MAKES 6 SERVINGS

If you are going to make the sauce from scratch, use the milk infusion from the smoked haddock instead of the fish stock in the recipe. If you have the sauce on hand, soak an extra pound of fish and use the soaking liquid from this recipe to make a soup with some extra sorrel sauce.

1 pound smoked haddock (finnan haddie)	2 tablespoons snipped fresh chives
2 cups milk	1/4 teaspoon salt
1 nonstick cooking spray	1/4 teaspoon freshly ground pepper
6 eggs, separated	Sorrel Cream Sauce, warm (see page 82)

■ Combine fish and milk in small saucepan and heat to boiling over medium-high heat. Reduce heat to low and simmer 15 minutes; until fish starts to separate. Drain, reserving liquid for another use.

■ Preheat oven to 350° F. Grease a deep 9-inch pie plate with nonstick cooking spray. Spread haddock over bottom of dish.

■ Whisk egg yolks, chives, salt, and pepper in deep medium bowl until blended. Beat the egg whites until soft peaks form when the beaters are raised. Fold the egg whites into egg-yolk mixture with a rubber spatula; spread evenly into the prepared dish. Bake 15 to 20 minutes, until a knife inserted near the center comes out clean. Cut omelet into wedges; serve with the sauce.

Without sauce: 212 calories; 4 g carbohydrates, 28 g protein, 6 g fat

Clam Quiche with a Cheese Crust

MAKES 6 SERVINGS

Long Island's clam pies are encased in potatoes and pastry. This recipe is for when you hanker for the filling and not a lot of carbs.

Nonstick cooking spray for greasing pie plate
8 (1/2-ounce) thick slices domestic muenster cheese
4 eggs, beaten until smooth
4 thick slices bacon, fried until crisp but not hard, chopped
2 marinated sun-dried tomato, finely chopped

1 1/2 cups shucked cherrystone or chowder clams, chopped medium fine
1/2 cup shredded extra-sharp cheddar cheese
1/2 cup half-and-half or cream
1/4 teaspoon freshly ground pepper
1/8 teaspoon garlic powder
pinch of cayenne pepper

■ Preheat oven to 325° F. Grease a deep, 9-inch glass pie plate with cooking spray. Line with cheese slices, overlapping slightly, keeping slices long around the edges and cutting to fit along the sides. Lightly press overlapping pieces together.

■ Place eggs in large bowl; whisk until smooth. Stir in bacon, tomato, clams, cheese, half-and-half, pepper, garlic powder, and cayenne. Pour into lined pie plate. Bake 20 to 30 minutes, until set but not bubbling in the center. Place on wire rack; cool to room temperature before cutting. Serve while warm.

Per Serving: 424 calories; 3 g carbohydrates, 25 g protein, 34 g fat

Spinach and Preserved Lemon Soufflés

The combination of eggs and lemons is brought to new heights in this airy dish. Make it an appetizer in little dishes, a first course in slightly larger dishes, or a lunch main course in a single communal bowl. It's French with an African twist, perfect for an après *Casablanca* matinee.

2 tablespoons unsalted butter for greasing dish	**1/4 cup chopped Preserved Lemons, (see page 99)**
almond flour for dusting dishes	**4 egg yolks**
Steakhouse Creamed Spinach, warm, not hot, (see page 182)	**6 egg whites**
	1/4 teaspoon cream of tartar

▪ Grease 8 (6-ounce) ramekins with half the butter. Refrigerate 20 minutes and repeat; sprinkle the dishes with flour and refrigerate.

▪ Preheat oven to 350° F. Place Steakhouse Creamed Spinach and Preserved Lemons in large bowl; stir in egg yolks.

▪ Beat egg whites with cream of tartar until stiff peaks form. Fold 1/4 of the beaten egg whites into spinach mixture. Fold in remainder of beaten egg whites. Spoon mixture into prepared ramekins; bake 25 minutes, until a thin metal tester or toothpick comes out clean. Serve the soufflés immediately.

Per serving: 234 calories; 5 g carbohydrates, 13 g protein, 19 g fat

Open-Face Vegetable-Bin Omelet

MAKES 3 TO 4 SERVINGS

When you look in the fridge and it's eggs or nothing for dinner, the saving grace can be what lies in the crisper. A little of a lot of vegetables goes a long way when you arrange everything in a single layer in the eggs, and it looks pretty, too.

6 eggs

2 tablespoons butter

2 tablespoons olive oil

4 radishes, cut crosswise into 1/4 inch thick rounds

4 green onions, trimmed and chopped

1 Kirby cucumber, peeled, seeded and diced

1 jalapeno pepper, seeded if desired, finely chopped

1 red bell pepper, seeded, julienned

1/2 cup finely shredded cabbage

1 large garlic clove, crushed to a paste through a press

1/4 cup loosely packed fresh cilantro leaves, chopped

1/2 teaspoon salt

1/4 teaspoon freshly ground pepper

■ Preheat broiler. Melt butter in oil over medium-high heat in 10-inch heavy skillet with heat-resistant handle. Add radishes, onions, and peppers; sauté 3 minutes, until softened. Add cabbage; sauté 2 minutes. Add garlic; sauté 1 minute or until all vegetables are tender. Reduce heat to medium-low.

■ Lightly whisk eggs, salt, and pepper in a large bowl until mixed; stir in cilantro and pour mixture over vegetables. Cook, lifting vegetables so eggs can slide underneath. When almost set on bottom, broil 2 minutes, until top is set but still moist. Serve at once.

Each of 3 servings: 335 calories; 9 g carbohydrates, 14 g protein, 27 g fat

Vegetables

Pumpkin with Dill and Egg Sauce and Toasted Pumpkin Seeds

MAKES 6 SERVINGS

Pick a special eating pumpkin, and this dish will really dazzle. You can toast and shell and retoast the seeds that are in the pumpkin or buy already shelled seeds at a health foods store.

Spicy Pumpkin Seeds
2 tablespoons green pumpkin seeds
1 teaspoon olive oil
1/2 teaspoon salt
1/4 teaspoon ground cumin
1/4 teaspoon chili powder
11/2-pound piece seeded sugar pumpkin, peeled, cut into 3/4-inch cubes
1/4 cup butter

2/3 cup minced onion
2 hard-cooked eggs, peeled and finely chopped
2 tablespoons minced fresh dill
2 tablespoons minced fresh parsley
1 teaspoon salt
1/4 teaspoon freshly ground white pepper

▨ Preheat oven to 350° F. Place pumpkin seeds on parchment-lined baking sheet; drizzle with oil, salt, cumin, and chili powder. Toss to coat; spread out. Bake 8 to 10 minutes, until crisp. Cool and set aside.

▨ Place pumpkin pieces in a single layer in a shallow glass baking dish with enough water to come 1/4 inch up sides of dish; cover with plastic wrap and microwave on HIGH 10 minutes, until tender. Let stand, covered, 5 minutes. Meanwhile, melt butter in medium skillet over medium-high heat; add onion and sauté 5 minutes, until tender. Add eggs, dill, parsley, salt, and pepper; mix. Heat through.

▨ Drain pumpkin, reserving 1/2 cup cooking liquid; place in warm serving bowl. Stir enough cooking liquid into egg mixture to make a spoonable sauce: pour it over pumpkin. Sprinkle with pumpkin seeds; serve immediately.

Per serving: 138 calories; 10 g carbohydrates, 5 g protein, 12 g fat

(See overleaf for recipe photo)

Spicy Braised Greens

This nutritious side dish goes with everything. I've often sprinkled a bowl of leftovers with chopped hard-cooked eggs for a healthy lunch. After that, if there was some left, it went into a pot of soup.

1 pound rinsed, trimmed kale, mustard greens, escarole, or endive
¼ cup your best extra-virgin olive oil plus more for drizzling
4 large cloves garlic, peeled and sliced

1 teaspoon crushed red-pepper flakes
1 cup hot vegetable broth, chicken broth, or water
salt to taste

▪ Break or cut leaves into 2-inch pieces. Rinse well again and drain.

▪ Heat ¼ cup oil in a large, deep skillet or saucepan over medium-high heat and add garlic and pepper flakes. (Avert your nose because the pepper flakes will send up a sinus-cleaning draft!) Cook just until garlic is fragrant. Add broth; heat to boiling. Add greens; stir until wilted. Cover almost completely and cook 20 minutes, until greens are tender and most of the liquid has evaporated. (Remove lid after 15 minutes if greens are tender so the liquid can concentrate.) Season with salt; drizzle with olive oil.

Per serving: 130 calories; 8 g carbohydrates, 3 g protein, 10 g fat

Steakhouse Creamed Spinach

MAKES 4 SERVINGS

Here is a classic side dish that never fails to make that steak next to it a little sexier!

2 (10-ounce) bags fresh spinach or 1 (10-ounce) box frozen chopped spinach
2 tablespoons unsalted butter
1/2 cup minced onions
1 (8-ounce) package cream cheese, softened, in chunks

2 tablespoons heavy cream
fresh lemon juice to taste
pinch of freshly grated nutmeg or to taste
kosher salt and freshly ground pepper to taste

■ Rinse spinach well and remove stems; drain in colander but don't spin dry. Place in large pot with the water still on the leaves. Cover; heat to boiling over medium heat. Steam 5 minutes, stirring down uncooked spinach, every minute or so, until all the spinach is wilted and dark green, not brown. Or, cook frozen spinach as package label directs. Drain, pressing out water.

■ Melt butter in a large skillet over medium heat. When foaming subsides, add onion; sauté until soft, about 4 minutes. Stir in cream cheese, heating until melted. Add spinach, cream, and nutmeg and season with lemon juice, salt, and pepper. Cook just until hot.

Per serving: 289 calories; 9 g carbohydrates, 9 g protein, 26 g fat

Chunky Parsnips with Saffron and Lemon

MAKES 4 TO 6 SERVINGS

By making each piece fuller flavored, a few make the perfect serving size. Saffron tints the pale parsnips a royal gold color and lemon adds a sunny presence.

9 ounces (about 2 large) parsnips, peeled and cut into 1-inch chunks

1/2 teaspoon salt and more to taste

1 cup heavy cream

1/2 teaspoon saffron threads

2 teaspoons grated lemon zest

2 teaspoon fresh lemon juice

freshly ground white pepper to taste

■ Place parsnips in medium saucepan, cover with water, and add a 1/2 teaspoon salt. Cover; heat to boiling over medium-high heat. Simmer 20 minutes, until tender when pierced with a paring knife.

■ Meanwhile, heat cream to boiling in small saucepan; simmer over low heat until reduced by half. Remove from heat. Place saffron in custard cup and crush with back of a spoon. Stir into cream; cover and let steep 10 minutes.

■ Drain parsnips; add cream, lemon zest, lemon juice, and salt and pepper to taste. Stir gently to coat. Place in serving bowl.

Each of 6 servings: 87 calories; 9 g carbohydrates, 1 g protein, 6 g fat

Cauliflower "Mashed Potatoes"

MAKES 2 TO 4 SERVINGS

Even a healthy pile of these "spuds" won't dent your diet. The amount and importance of the visual and sensory satisfaction this dish adds to a low-carb plate is not to be underestimated. Every forkful should be a revelation!

**1/4 cup heavy cream or more if
    needed**

1 tablespoon butter

**1/2 pound cauliflower florets
    with stems**

salt to taste

Heat cream and butter to boiling in medium saucepan. Add cauliflower; sprinkle with salt. Cook, stirring, 10 minutes, until cauliflower is tender. Puree in pan with hand-held blender or in processor.

Each of 2 servings: 118 calories; 7 g carbohydrates, 3 g protein, 9 g fat

Leek and Prosciutto Gratin

MAKES 4 SERVINGS

This is so easy to make! You can leave out the ham and even the cheese, and still have a tasty side dish.

3 small leeks or large green onions

2 ounces paper-thin slices
   prosciutto

1 cup heavy cream

1/4 teaspoon salt

1/4 teaspoon freshly ground
   pepper or to taste

1 cup shredded asiago cheese

■ Preheat oven to 375° F. Trim ends and tough green portions from leeks. Quarter leeks lengthwise, rinse very well under running water to remove grit. Place in 2-quart gratin or baking dish. Cut prosciutto crosswise into 1/2 inch thick slices; sprinkle over leeks. Pour cream over all; sprinkle with salt, pepper, and cheese. Bake 35 minutes, until leeks are tender and cream has been absorbed, basting every 10 minutes or so with cream.

Per serving: 172 calories; 9 g carbohydrates, 10 g protein, 11 g fat

Creamed Broccoli with Ginger

SERVES 6 TO 8

I thought this was tasty but wondered how my dinner guests would like it. It turned out to be a big hit!

1¹/2 teaspoons extra-virgin olive oil
1/4-inch slice peeled fresh ginger
1 medium onion, thinly sliced
1 large clove garlic, crushed
   through a press
1/2 cup heavy cream

2 pounds broccoli, trimmed into
   florets with 1 inch of the stem
1/2 to 1 teaspoon ginger juice
   (bottled or squeezed from
   fresh ginger)
salt and cayenne pepper to taste

■ Heat oil in large nonstick saucepan over medium heat. Add ginger slice and onion; cover. Cook 5 minutes. Add garlic; cook 1 minute longer. Add cream, heat to boiling, and simmer 4 minutes to thicken slightly. Discard ginger slice; keep cream mixture warm.

■ Cook broccoli in large pan of boiling, salted water 8 to 10 minutes, until very tender. Drain, press out excess water, and chop in food processor. Add cream mixture, 1/2 teaspoon ginger juice and a pinch each salt and cayenne; pulse to make a rough puree. Taste, adjust seasoning, and serve warm.

Each of 6 servings: 86 calories; 10 g carbohydrates, 5 g protein, 4 g fat

Fennel Purée with Mascarpone

MAKES 4 SERVINGS

If you can have cauliflower and broccoli purees, do you need another? Well, fennel is licorice-flavored and goes beautifully with fish and grilled dishes.

2 medium fennel bulbs
1/4 cup butter
1/2 teaspoon salt and more to taste

1 (8-ounce) container mascarpone
fresh lemon juice to taste
freshly ground pepper to taste

▓ Cut off fennel stalks; coarsely chop fern and reserve. Dice bulbs into rough 1/2-inch dice. Melt butter in large nonstick skillet over medium-high heat; add fennel, sprinkle with salt, and sauté 3 minutes, until glistening and fragrant. Add 1/2 cup water, cover, and steam over medium heat 20 minutes, until crisp-tender. Remove lid and simmer until liquid has evaporated and fennel is soft.

▓ Place fennel in food processor; add mascarpone. Puree; return to skillet to heat through. Season with salt, lemon juice, and pepper. Stir in fennel fern.

Per serving: 254 calories; 10 g carbohydrates, 3 g protein, 24g fat

Sherried Mushooms with Toasted Walnuts

MAKES 4 SERVINGS

This Spanish side dish will not fail to support hearty main dishes like grilled kidneys, liver, or steak.

2 tablespoons butter
1 tablespoon extra-virgin olive oil, preferably Spanish
8 ounces fresh mushrooms, quartered
2 tablespoons dry sherry
1 tablespoon fresh lemon juice

1 tablespoon grated orange or lemon zest
fine sea salt to taste
$1/2$ cup chopped toasted walnuts
2 tablespoons chopped fresh parsley

▪ Melt butter in oil in large skillet over medium-high heat. Add mushrooms; sauté 5 minutes, until tender. Stir in sherry, lemon juice, and zest; cook 1 minute. Season with salt; stir in walnuts and parsley.

Per serving: 189 calories; 5 g carbohydrates, 4 g protein, 18 g fat

Stir-Fried Asparagus with Garlic and Almonds

MAKES 6 SERVINGS

In the throes of asparagus season last spring I got pretty fussy about eating the stringy stalks. Every time I cooked a bunch, I just whacked off the tips, served them, and froze the stalks into a zip-top bag. Come summer, I made some wonderful asparagus soup from my fussy frugalness. So you can make this dish with 3 bunches of asparagus tips, freeze the tough portions of the stalks, and do the same.

3 tablespoons peanut oil or
   vegetable oil
2 cloves garlic, crushed through
   a garlic press
1 teaspoon salt
pinch of sugar

2 tablespoons water
2 tablespoons soy sauce
2 (1-pound) bunches fresh
   asparagus, trimmed and cut
   into 1-inch pieces
1/2 cup sliced almonds, toasted

■ Heat a wok or large skillet over high heat and add oil, garlic, salt, and sugar. Stir-fry 1 minute, until fragrant. Add water and heat to boiling. Add asparagus and stir-fry 2 minutes. Add soy sauce, cover, and steam 3 minutes, until crisp-tender. Remove cover and cook until liquid has evaporated. Turn out onto a serving platter. Sprinkle with almonds.

Per serving: 172 calories; 10 g carbohydrates, 6 g protein, 13 g fat

Balsamic-Glazed Brussels Sprouts with Hazelnuts

MAKES 4 TO 6 SERVINGS

In a marriage of blue bloods, sweet, rich balsamic vinegar happily unites with the bold, earthy hazelnut oil. Try it with asparagus or green beans, and add julienned red bell pepper for color.

1 pound fresh small brussels
  sprouts trimmed
1 tablespoon hazelnut oil or
  to taste
1 1/2 teaspoons extra-virgin
  olive oil

1/2 teaspoon salt or to taste
1/4 teaspoon freshly ground
  pepper or to taste
2 tablespoons balsamic vinegar
1/4 cup hazelnuts, toasted,
  skinned and chopped

■ Place sprouts in a large bowl, sprinkle with 1 tablespoon hazelnut oil, salt, and pepper, and toss to coat. Heat oil and 2 tablespoons water to boiling in large nonstick skillet over medium-high heat; add sprouts. Cover; cook 5 minutes. Add vinegar; reduce heat to medium. Cover; cook 10 minutes, until sprouts are tender. Uncover; cook until liquid evaporates, basting every 3 minutes.

■ Taste sprouts; adjust hazelnut oil, salt, and pepper if needed. Place on serving platter; sprinkle with hazelnuts.

Each of 6 servings Brussels sprouts: 123 calories; 8 g carbohydrates, 4 g protein, 10 g fat

Roasted Green Beans with Orange and Mint

MAKES 6 SERVINGS

An interesting way to meld flavors is by cooking these alongside any kind of meat or fish in one pan to meld the flavors.

1 1/2 pounds fresh green beans, trimmed, cut into 2-inch pieces
1/3 cup extra-virgin olive oil
2 large shallots, thinly sliced
fine sea salt to taste

freshly ground pepper to taste
1 to 2 tablespoon chopped fresh mint, to taste
1 teaspoon grated orange zest

■ Preheat oven to 450° F. Place beans in roasting pan.

■ Heat oil in small skillet over medium-high heat; sauté shallots 3 minutes, until tender. Pour oil and shallots over beans; sprinkle with salt and pepper and toss to coat. Roast 15 minutes, until beans are tender but not soft, stirring once.

■ Sprinkle 1 tablespoon mint and the zest over beans; toss to mix. Taste for seasonings and adjust if necessary. Place on platter.

Per serving: 152 calories; 10 g carbohydrates, 2 g protein, 13 g fat

Spicy Parsnip Oven Fries

MAKES 8 SERVINGS

Little sticks of salty vegetable nibbles are sorely missed on a low-carb diet. You can have these, as a French-fry substitute, if you don't eat the whole batch at one seating!

1 pound parsnips, peeled
2 tablespoons olive oil

1 tablespoon Cajun Spice Rub,
 (see page 98)

▦ Preheat oven to 425° F. Cut parsnips into French-fry size pieces. Place in bowl; toss with oil. Sprinkle with spice mix; toss again. Spread out on nonstick baking sheet. Bake, stirring occasionally, 20 to 25 minutes, until tender inside and crisp outside.

Per serving: 104 calories; 10 g carbohydrates, 1 g protein, 7 g fat

Eggplant with Smoked Mozzarella and Almonds

MAKES 4 SERVINGS

I use a wonderful smoked mozzarella to make this; the flavor is fabulous with eggplant and almonds.

olive oil for greasing the baking
  dish
1 pound eggplant, peeled, cut
  into ¹/₂-inch cubes
2 thin slices onion
12 lightly toasted blanched
  almonds

salt
4 ounces smoked mozzarella,
  sliced
1 tablespoon freshly grated
  asiago or other hard cheese
freshly ground pepper to taste
ground allspice to taste

▓ Preheat oven to 350° F. Oil a 1¹/₂-quart shallow baking dish.

▓ Cook eggplant and onion in a large skillet with 1 cup boiling water over medium heat, 8 to 10 minutes, just until tender. Remove eggplant with slotted spoon to prepared baking dish; reserve broth and onions.

▓ Place almonds in blender or food processor; process until finely chopped. With motor running, add ¹/₂ cup water from cooking the eggplant and the onions. Process until smooth. Season with salt; pour over the eggplant. Cover with mozzarella; sprinkle with asiago, pepper, and allspice. Bake 20 minutes, until mozzarella melts and eggplant is hot.

Per serving: 143 calories; 9 g carbohydrates, 9 g protein, 9 g fat

Pisto Manchego
(Spanish Squash and Egg Stew)

MAKES 6 SERVINGS

The origins of this colorful, ratatouille-like mix of vegetables is La Mancha, the land of Don Quixote. It is usually served with roasted meat, but can itself be a main course if ham or bacon is added. There are endless variations; this one is the one I like best.

3 tablespoons olive oil
1 large Spanish onion, coarsely chopped
2 large cloves garlic, minced
2 medium zucchini, chopped into 1/2-inch cubes
3 cups coarsely chopped seeded, peeled tomatoes (fresh or canned)

1 teaspoon salt or to taste
1/2 teaspoon freshly ground pepper or to taste
1 egg, lightly beaten
1 hard-cooked egg, the white cut lengthwise into 1/4-inch strips and the yolks crumbled with a fork

■ Heat oil in a large heavy skillet over medium-high heat. Add onion; sauté 7 minutes, until softened. Add garlic; sauté 30 seconds. Stir in zucchini, tomatoes, salt and pepper. Cover; reduce heat to medium-low. Simmer, 30 minutes, stirring often, adding about 1/4 cup water during cooking to keep mixture from sticking to pan.

■ When the vegetables are tender and the mixture is a chunky puree, taste and adjust the seasoning if necessary. Add the beaten egg, stirring constantly to mix with all the vegetables; and pour into a serving bowl. Sprinkle with the hard-cooked egg.

Per serving: 130 calories; 10 g carbohydrates, 4 g protein, 9 g fat

Southern Summer Squash Casserole

SERVES 4

The cracker-topped, full-carb original recipe of this adaptation is one of my three favorite ways to have yellow squash. (The others are my Mom's, simmered with a little water, salt and pepper and lots of butter, and another southern version, pan-fried in bacon fat with lots of onions until soft.) Even without the topping, though, this is wonderful!

1 pound yellow summer squash or zucchini or a mixture of both

3 tablespoons butter plus extra for greasing dish

1/2 cup onion, chopped

1 garlic, crushed through a garlic press

1/2 red bell pepper, seeded and chopped

1/2 green bell pepper, seeded and chopped

1 hot red chile or jalapeño pepper, seeded and chopped (optional)

2 large eggs, beaten

1/2 cup heavy cream

1/2 teaspoon salt

1 cup grated extra-sharp yellow cheddar cheese

hot paprika or chili powder for sprinkling

■ Preheat oven to 350° F. Butter a 1¹/2-quart baking dish and set aside. Place a large pot of salted water on to boil. Scrub, trim and slice squash and cut into 1/2 inch thick slices. Add to boiling water and cook until tender, about 10 minutes. Drain, puree in food processor, and pour into a large bowl.

■ Melt 3 tablespoons butter over medium heat. Add onion, garlic, and peppers and cook until just tender, about 5 minutes. Add to squash mixture. Stir in eggs, cream, and seasonings. Blend well and pour into prepared baking dish. Top with cheese, sprinkle with paprika, and bake 20 minutes, until bubbly and cheese melts.

Per serving: 368 calories; 10 g carbohydrates, 13 g protein, 32 g fat

Zucchini and Garlic Pancakes

MAKES 8 PANCAKES

These smell so great when you are frying them and they are so easy to eat!

2 (6-ounce) zucchini
2 large garlic cloves, crushed
    through a press
1/2 teaspoon dried oregano
1/4 teaspoon freshly ground pepper

1/8 to 1/4 teaspoon kosher salt
1 teaspoon flour
olive oil for frying
1/4 cup freshly grated Parmesan
    cheese

■ Peel the zucchini; shred into long strands onto a clean tea towel. Roll up the strands in the towel; twist over the sink to extract as much liquid as possible. Place zucchini in a bowl. Add oregano, garlic, pepper and salt; toss with a fork until mixed. Sprinkle with the flour; toss to mix.

■ Pour enough oil into a large nonstick skillet to cover the bottom (about 4 tablespoons for a 10-inch skillet) and heat over medium-high heat until almost smoking. Making 4 pancakes at a time, spoon zucchini mixture into the skillet in 1 tablespoon patties and flatted into lacy 3-inch rounds with the back of a fork. Fry until crisp and golden brown in the center, 3 to 4 minutes on each side. Drain on paper towels and keep warm while frying the remaining pancakes. Sprinkle with cheese before serving.

Per 1 pancake: 35 calories; 2 g carbohydrates, 2 g protein, 3 g fat

Grilled Radicchio with Vegetable Pesto

MAKES 4 SERVINGS

That red stuff in salad mixes that isn't cabbage changes personality when it is grilled. The bitterness softens and is soothed further when the sweet mozzarella melts and oozes into every juicy, delightfully squishy bite.

2 medium heads radicchio
(1 pound total)
3 oil-packed sun-dried tomatoes, chopped
4 ounces whole-milk mozzarella cheese, shredded

2 tablespoons salted capers, rinsed, dried, chopped
2 tablespoons Vegetable Kale Pesto, (see page 96), or other pesto
2 tablespoons balsamic vinegar
oil for brushing packets

■ Preheat outdoor grill for barbecue or preheat broiler. Remove 4 large leaves from radicchio heads; reserve. Cut heads in half through cores; blanch removed leaves and halves in saucepan of boiling water 1 minute, until wilted. Drain in colander; cool.

■ Mix cheese, capers, Pesto, and vinegar in medium bowl; pat between radicchio layers. Wrap a blanched leaf around each half; secure with short metal skewers or wooden ones that have been soaked 20 minutes in water. Brush packets with oil; place on grill or broiler pan. Grill 6 inches from heat source, 10 minutes, until lightly browned and cheese inside has melted, basting with oil and turning them with long-handled tongs every couple minutes. If they brown too quickly, move them to a cooler part of the grill.

Per serving: 183 calories; 8 g carbohydrates, 9 g protein, 8 g fat

Desserts

Seckel Pears Poached in Lemongrass Syrup

MAKES 4 SERVINGS

These sweetest and sweetest-looking pears, developed by an 18th-century Pennsylvania farmer named Seckel, don't need sugar syrup for poaching. Instead, a little lemon and some supporting fruits for color, make this a refreshing finish to a meal.

Lemongrass Syrup:
1 1/2 cups water, divided
2 tablespoons dried cherries or
  cranberries
1 tablespoon dried blueberries

1/4 cup finely chopped lemongrass
  from inner leaves
2 (4-ounce) Seckle pears, halved
  or quartered lengthwise
shredded lemon zest for garnish

■ Place berries in a small bowl; pour 1/2 cup boiling water on top. Let steep 10 minutes, until plumped. Drain soaking liquid into small saucepan or sauté pan just wide enough to hold pears. Add remaining water and lemongrass; heat to boiling over medium heat; cover and simmer 10 minutes. Add pears; cover and simmer 7 to 10 minutes, basting with bulb baster every 5 minutes, until paring knife inserts easily in pears but pears are not soft enough to fall apart. Remove from heat; uncover, and let pears cool in liquid.

■ To serve: Carefully remove pears and cooking liquid to shallow bowls. Sprinkle cherries, blueberries, and lemon zest over pears.

Per serving: 38 calories, 10 g carbohydrates, trace protein, trace fat

(See overleaf for recipe photo)

Demi Meyer-Lemon Cheesecakes

MAKES 4 SERVINGS

These wonderfully sweet lemons are fun to use because they have the bite, flavor, and aroma of "ordinary" lemons but without sourness. The lemons offer the bright flavor, but the real backbone of these treats is the sweet richness of freshly made ricotta cheese.

1 cup fresh ricotta cheese
1/4 to 1/2 cup Meyer lemon juice
2 tablespoons sugar
2 to 3 tablespoons grated Meyer
   lemon zest

1 egg
finely slivered fresh mint for
   garnish

▨ Preheat oven to 325° F. Whisk cheese, 1/4 cup juice, the sugar, and 2 tablespoons zest in a bowl until smooth. Taste; adjust juice and zest amounts to make a smooth texture and assertive but pleasant lemon flavor.

▨ Whisk in egg; spoon into 4 Chinese teacups, espresso cups, or 4-ounce ramekins. Place on small baking sheet; bake 15 minutes, until knife inserted in centers comes out clean.

▨ Cool cheesecakes at least 1 hour; serve at room temperature or chilled. Garnish with mint before serving.

Per serving: 155 calories, 10 g carbohydrates, 9 g protein, 9 g fat

Meringue Nests with Grilled Grapefruit Eggs

MAKES 4 SERVINGS

Unfortunately you can't make meringues on a damp day; they won't stay crisp or poofy, for that matter. You can freeze them, though, so think ahead under sunny skies.

1 egg white, at room temperature
pinch of salt
pinch of cream of tartar
2 tablespoons plus 1 teaspoon
sugar

4 teaspoons slivered almonds
8 sections ruby grapefruit

■ Preheat oven to 250° F. Line a small baking sheet with parchment.

■ Beat egg white and salt in bowl with mixer at high speed. Beat in cream of tartar. Beat in 2 tablespoons sugar at high speed, 1 tablespoon at a time, beating well after each addition, until meringue is stiff. Spoon meringue into 4 high piles onto parchment-lined baking sheet; sprinkle with almonds. Make a 2-inch crater in each nest with back of spoon; press lightly to glue nuts to surface, not submerge them, to resemble twigs. Bake 1 hour or until shells are crisp; let stand in oven several hours to dry out completely. Store in airtight container.

■ Preheat broiler. Line small baking sheet with foil. Pat grapefruit dry with paper towel; place on foil on baking sheet. Sprinkle with 1 teaspoon sugar; broil until sugar caramelizes. Arrange 2 grapefruit "eggs" in each nest.

Per serving: 59 calories, 10 g carbohydrates, 2 g protein, 1 g fat

Pomegranate Panna Cotta

MAKES 4 SERVINGS

The joy of pomegranates is their ancient seasonal heritage, from myth to reality. If there is one fall tradition that you may want to start in your family, it's the awareness of the pomegranate. To make life easier, cut the fruit in half and place the cut side of one half facing into a bowl. Hit it from the backside with a wooden spoon to knock out the seeds.

1 cup heavy cream	**1 tablespoon unflavored gelatin**
1/2 cup milk	**1 teaspoon orange flower water**
1 tablespoon honey	**1/3 cup pomegranate seeds**
2 (3-inch) cinnamon sticks	**1 teaspoon finely shredded**
4 cloves	**orange zest for garnish**

▓ Heat cream, milk, honey, cinnamon sticks, and cloves to simmering in saucepan over medium heat. Cool; cover and refrigerate overnight.

▓ Next day: Strain cream mixture into clean saucepan; heat until hot but not boiling. Soak gelatin in 1 1/2 tablespoons water until soft; stir into cream mixture until dissolved. Let cool. Pour into glass measure; chill 20 minutes, until thickened. Stir in orange flower water and pomegranate seeds. Pour into shallow glass bowls. Chill at least 4 hours, until set. Sprinkle with zest before serving.

Per serving: 119 calories, 10 g carbohydrates, 4 g protein, 8 g fat

Kaffir Lime Custards

The floral aroma and flavor of these small leaves, grown in Asia and Hawaii, adds more exotic interest than your usual lime. They are available fresh, frozen, and dried, usually in Thai grocery stores; if you buy fresh ones, freeze or dry the ones leftover for steeping into coconut milk for soups and sauces.

1 cup heavy cream
1 cup coconut milk or plain milk
2 tablespoons palm sugar or
   brown sugar
1/2 vanilla bean
6 double fresh kaffir lime leaves or
   1 tablespoon grated lime zest
4 egg yolks

■ Heat cream, milk, sugar, vanilla bean, and lime leaves in small saucepan until steaming over low heat; cover and set aside to steep 1 hour. Heat again until steaming. Whisk egg yolks in medium bowl until blended; whisk in hot cream mixture.

■ Scrape out seeds from vanilla bean and whisk into custard so that seeds are separated. Strain into glass measure. Pour into 6 (4-ounce) ramekins. Place in steamer basket and steam over boiling water 5 to 7 minutes, until custards are set. Serve warm or chilled.

Per serving: 139 calories, 10 g carbohydrates, 4 g protein, 9 g fat

Ice Cream Finger Sandwiches

Work quickly so the gelato mixture will be creamy, not liquid, when you mix it with the mascarpone. The idea is to have wafer-thin cookies sandwiching your tablespoonful taste of gelato.

1 cup gelato, slightly softened
3 tablespoons mascarpone

36 thin Swedish gingersnaps or Moravian ginger cookies, or thin vanilla wafers

▨ Mix gelato and mascarpone quickly until swirled. Place on parchment and roll up into a cylinder slightly smaller than the diameter of the cookies. Freeze until firm.

▨ Cut roll into thirds. Working with one roll at a time, unroll gelato mixture; quickly cut into 6 equal slices. Sandwich each between 2 cookies with flat sides facing in. Freeze while repeating with remaining rolls and cookies. Serve immediately or place in plastic freezer container and freeze until serving.

Note: The gelato and mascarpone mixture may not freeze into a completely solid block which might make slicing a bit messy—but do the best that you can!

Per serving: 66 calories, 10 g carbohydrates, 1 g protein, 3 g fat

Plantation Chocolate Pots de Crème

MAKES 6 SERVINGS

From Venezuela to Madagascar, grow the tropical evergreen cacao tree, the source of all things chocolate grown on plantations. But now, small-batch boutique chocolates are some of the finest chocolates most of the world has ever tasted. As with coffee, each country has unique growing conditions and each producer, processing secrets that contribute to their fame. This "nothing but chocolate" lightly sweetened custard is the perfect medium to explore a new frontier of flavor.

4 ounces bittersweet plantation chocolate
1 tablespoon sugar

1 3/4 cups heavy cream
3 large egg yolks

■ Day before serving: Preheat oven to 325° F. Combine chocolate, sugar, and heavy cream in a medium saucepan and heat over low heat, whisking constantly, until the chocolate melts and mixture is smooth.

■ Mix egg yolks in medium bowl; gradually whisk in hot chocolate mixture.

■ Pour custard into 6 (4-ounce) sake cups or ramekins placed in a shallow roasting pan. Place pan on center oven rack. Pour enough hot water into pan to come halfway up the sides of the dishes. Bakes until the custards are set, 40 to 45 minutes.

■ Remove pots de crème from the roasting pan; cool on a wire rack. Cover loosely with plastic wrap; refrigerate overnight.

Per serving: 273 calories, 10 g carbohydrates, 5 g protein, 27 g fat

Passion-Fruit Bavarian

YIELD: 6 SERVINGS

1/2 cup fresh passion-fruit juice
or the pulp and juice of 3
large ripe passion fruits

3 allspice berries

2 egg yolks

2 1/2 tablespoons sugar

1 1/2 teaspoon unflavored gelatin

2 tablespoons cold water

oil or nonstick cooking spray

3/4 cup heavy cream

1 tablespoon grated lime zest

pulp and seeds from 2 passion
fruit for garnish

■ Heat fruit juice and allspice in small saucepan over low heat until hot.

■ Whisk egg yolks and sugar in a bowl until lemon-colored. Slowly beat in warm passion-fruit juice and allspice; place in top of double boiler over simmering water. Stir with a wooden spoon 15 minutes, until custard is hot and coats the back of the spoon. Remove from heat, strain into a mixing bowl, pressing on the passion-fruit pulp, if using, with the back of a spoon, and cool slightly.

■ Place water in a small bowl. Sprinkle gelatin on top; let soak 5 minutes. Add gelatin to custard; stir until completely dissolved. Place bowl of custard in a bigger bowl of ice water; stir until cool and almost set.

■ Lightly grease 6 (4-ounce) ramekins or other small molds or bowls with oil or nonstick cooking spray. Place heavy cream in a deep bowl and whip until peaks are firm but not stiff. Fold in lime zest and then fold whipped cream into custard. Pour into prepared molds and refrigerate until firm.

■ When ready to serve, pull the custard away from the sides of the molds with your thumb to break the suction. Invert onto a serving dishes and remove molds. Spoon passion fruit pulp on top of each serving.

Per serving: 94 calories, 10 g carbohydrates, 3 g protein, 5 g fat

Grilled Kelsey Plum Tarts with Pistachios

MAKES 8 SERVINGS

2/3 cup shelled natural (green) pistachios
1/2 cup butter, softened
2 tablespoons plus 1 teaspoon sugar
1 teaspoon vanilla extract

2 eggs
2 tablespoons almond flour
1 tablespoon all-purpose flour
nonstick cooking spray
2 Kelsey plums, halved, pitted

▦ Preheat oven to 400° F. Chop nuts in food processor; remove to bowl. Process butter, 2 tablespoons sugar, and vanilla in processor until smooth. Add nuts, eggs, and flour; pulse just until pastry comes together.

▦ Grease the inside of shallow tartlet pans or muffin pans with cooking spray; place on baking sheet. Pat pastry into each, dividing evenly. Bake 10 minutes, until golden and set.

▦ Preheat broiler. Cut plum halves into thin slices. Fan out slices on top of each tart. Sprinkle with remaining sugar; broil 5 inches from heat 3 to 4 minutes, until plums are charred, tender, and sizzling. Cool tarts slightly, carefully remove from pans and serve warm.

Per serving: 227 calories, 10 g carbohydrates, 5 g protein, 19 g fat

Star Anise-Mascarpone Semifreddo

MAKES 6 SERVINGS

A few spices charge the honey-sweetened cream with exotic interest. Serve "half-cold" as its name implies, so the flavorings are not masked by the cool temperature.

2 cups heavy cream, divided in 2
2 star anise
1 (3-inch) cinnamon stick
1 tablespoon dark, flavorful honey

1/4 teaspoon Chinese five-spice powder
1/2 cup mascarpone
1 to 2 star fruit (carambola), cut crosswise into slices (see serving note below

■ Mix 1 cup cream, spices, honey, and spice powder in small saucepan; heat to boiling over medium heat. Simmer 15 minutes, until cream is reduced by half. Set aside to cool.

■ Whip remaining cream in large, deep bowl until soft peaks form. Pour honey cream through sieve into another large bowl; discard spices. Add mascarpone; whisk until blended. Fold in the whipped cream using a rubber spatula. Spoon semifreddo into Chinese rice bowls. Cover and refrigerate; remove from refrigerator about 15 minutes before serving.

■ To serve: Slice star fruit crosswise so that you get 6 beautiful thin stars from the widest part of the fruit; cut the slice so that it can be hung over the side of the bowl and into each semifreddo as you would serve a slice of lemon on a glass of iced tea.

Per serving: 227 calories, 10 g carbohydrates, 5 g protein, 19 g fat

Coconut Ice with Figs

MAKES 6 SERVINGS

You want to use the instant coconut powder, not finely powdered or grated coconut, for this easy dessert. If figs aren't in season, serve the ice with a heavy downfall of toasted flakes of coconut.

1/2 cup instant coconut-cream powder	3 ripe figs
1/2 teaspoon pure almond extract	curry powder for dusting

■ Place coconut powder in small bowl; whisk in 1/2 cup warm water until blended. Whisk in almond extract. Pour in freezer-safe container; freeze, stirring frequently with fork to make texture smooth.

■ Cut figs lengthwise into 6 wedges; place scoops of ice in small shallow bowls and slide figs in next to them. Sprinkle ice with a small pinch of curry powder from on high so it spreads out.

Per serving: 206 calories, 10 g carbohydrates, 4 g protein, 17 g fat

Index

Acknowledgments

This book and my life would not be as interesting and beautiful without the inspiration of others. I am grateful to my family—my mother, Dorothy L. Johnson,my father, George P. Johnson, my four brothers and two sisters and their families and to the Stotzky family for their enthusiastic tasting and sustaining encouragement.

I thank Shirley Henkel, Rachel Sancilio, and "Mama Sue" Ralston for their kitchen wisdom. Thanks to *New York Times Magazine* food writers Julia Reed, Jason Epstein, Jonathan Reynolds, and Amanda Hesser and editors Michael Boodro and Maura Egan: Testing their recipes has enlarged my gastronomical world. Thanks to Bolo Restaurant for use of their beautiful tableware. And, thanks to Pamela Horn, my editor, for guidance, patience, and vision.